PRAISE FOR *FINANCIAL AUTONOMY*

'A clear, sensible and straightforward guide to taking control of your money and putting you on the path to financial independence.'

Stephen Miles, Investment Editor, *Sydney Morning Herald* and *The Age*

'Paul writes in a way that takes you from not knowing how or where to begin with money to having the confidence to make real changes after one reading session. The five steps outlined in this book are a testament to Paul's practical experience with helping hundreds of people, face-to-face over the years. Put simply, Paul knows what works and in what order. If you have no idea about your money life or perhaps are after some encouragement as your plans have drifted – this book is for you. For me, it is refreshing to read something easy to understand with lots of visual prompts and I'd encourage you to lean to the gold within.'

Glen James, My millennial money

'*Financial Autonomy* is a holistic guidebook to your financial future. Rather than just advising "how to invest" or "how to get rich", Paul outlines three distinct – but possibly overlapping – strategies to build wealth and freedom. Or choice. Or independence. Or autonomy. Most importantly, he'll help you analyse your true financial goals and needs to help you choose the right path for you.'

Nick Loper, The Side Hustle Show

'If you're looking for a digestible, results-driven book to take control of your finances, then this is the book for you. A must-read.'

Bryce Leske, Equity Mates

'As a young Australian, I strongly relate to Paul's message of taking back financial control over your life and know first-hand just how empowering it is to do so. Many people discuss shares and property as the way to reach financial independence, however Paul has started the conversation about a third way, starting a business. Paul has packed *Financial Autonomy* with fantastic examples of what this could look like and has the knowledge and experience to back it up. I would highly recommend *Financial Autonomy* to anyone looking to explore their options to regain control over their financial life.'

Kate Campbell, How to Money

'I have worked with Paul for over ten years to build my portfolio with a focus on my early retirement. Paul listens to my goals, which do change, and adjusts our approach as my needs adjust. Paul is patient and I rely on his sound financial advice.'

Emma-Louise Ward, Client of Guidance Financial Services

'I really enjoyed reading Paul's book. He made what can be complex financial concepts incredibly simple to understand. The book also covered a wide scope including investing in property, shares and even starting a business or side hustle, which is very valuable. Perhaps the thing I enjoyed the most was that *Financial Autonomy* was very practical and relatable with plenty of real-life examples, checklists and quizzes.'

Stuart Wemyss – Director, ProSolution Private Clients
and author of the best-selling *Investopoly*

FINANCIAL AUTONOMY

The money book that gives you choice

PAUL BENSON

First published in 2020 by Major Street Publishing Pty Ltd
E | info@majorstreet.com.au
W | majorstreet.com.au
M | +61 421 707 983

A catalogue record for this
book is available from the
National Library of Australia

NATIONAL
LIBRARY
OF AUSTRALIA

ISBN: 978-0-6487530-8-7

Cover design by Tess McCabe
Cover photograph by Melissa Martin
Internal design by Production Works
Printed in Australia by Ovato, an Accredited ISO AS/NZS 14001:2004
Environmental Management System Printer.

10 9 8 7 6 5 4 3 2 1

CONTENTS

A new focus   1

PART ONE: DEFINE SUCCESS   **11**
1. Goal-setting with purpose   13

PART TWO: CASH FLOW   **31**
2. Cash-flow mastery   33
3. Six strategies to maximise your savings   47

PART THREE: INVEST IN STOCKS   **67**
4. Stock market foundations   69
5. Investment selection and strategy   85

PART FOUR: INVEST IN PROPERTY   **103**
6. Property cash flow and debt   105
7. Property selection and strategy   125

PART FIVE: SELF-EMPLOYMENT   **145**
8. Side hustles, idea validation and strategy   147
9. Pricing, profit and money stuff   167

What about my retirement savings?   187
Action time   191
Want more?   197
About the author   199
Sources   201
Index   203

A NEW FOCUS

Plenty of books, podcasts and blogs focus on building wealth – and that's great, as far as it goes. But focusing just on wealth misses the point. I've worked with hundreds of people for over 20 years, helping them manage their financial lives, and my observation is that what we actually all want is something else. Being financially wealthy – rich in the classic Scrooge McDuck sense – is not the end point most of us seek.

What we're actually seeking is choice.

Choice in how much time we give to income-producing activities.

Choice about what those income-producing activities are.

Choice about where we live.

Choice about when we retire.

Choice about the ways we use our money to produce happiness.

That's why this book is called *Financial Autonomy*. It's not called *How to Make a Million Dollars*, or even the closely related but still not quite right *Financial Independence*.

I'm not promising to make you rich, though building wealth is often an important step to gaining choice. Instead, I'll focus on helping you determine what it is you're seeking, and then on developing your own personal roadmap to deliver that. Too many people aim at the wrong target – mostly, in my experience, not out of ignorance or foolishness, but because they are conforming to the standard narrative.

Do any of these goals seem familiar?

- 'Success in life is being able to retire as early as possible.'
- 'It's important that I update my car every four years.'
- 'If I don't work 40-plus hours per week, I'm a slacker.'
- 'The more stuff I have, the happier I'll be, and the happier I'll make those important to me.'

You've made the decision to pick up and read a book called *Financial Autonomy*, which suggests to me that you're already questioning these sorts of standard goals that we're led to believe should be the focus of our lives. You're not alone. I've been producing a podcast, unsurprisingly called *Financial Autonomy*, for three years now, and thousands of people just like you listen in each week.

The truth is:

- Retiring early with nothing to fill your days leads to a miserable, lonely life.

- Your ten-year-old car will get you where you need to go perfectly well, provided it's well maintained.

- The number of hours you devote to generating income should be determined by how much income you need to live the life that works for you, not by some sort of societal prescription.

- As the growing minimalist movement has found, less stuff rather than more stuff can make us happier, and is also a whole lot better for our planet.

THE JOURNEY TO FINANCIAL AUTONOMY

I'm a visual thinker – when I've got a problem that I need to think through I go to the whiteboard. Here's how I think about the journey to financial autonomy.

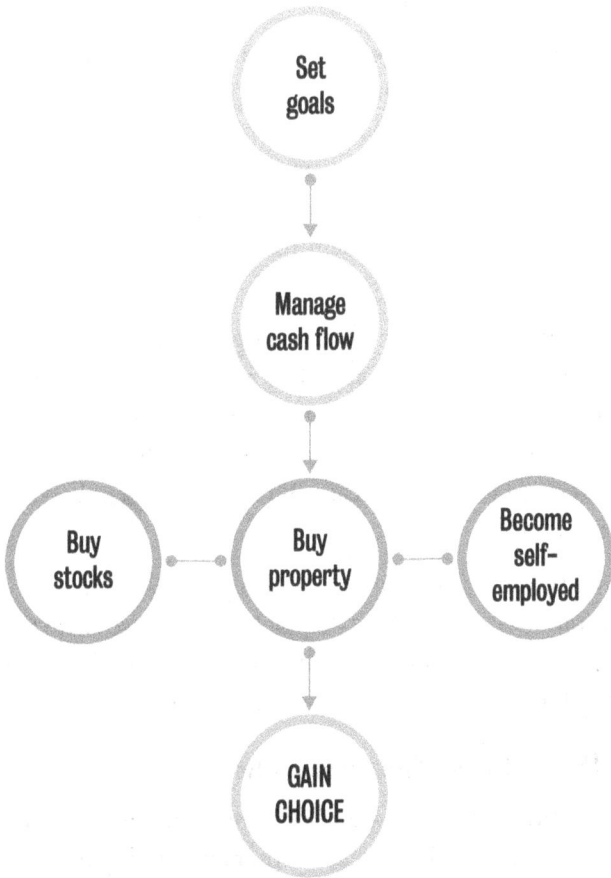

```
        ┌──────────┐
        │   Set    │
        │  goals   │
        └────┬─────┘
             │
             ▼
        ┌──────────┐
        │  Manage  │
        │ cash flow│
        └────┬─────┘
             │
             ▼
┌────────┐ ┌──────────┐ ┌──────────┐
│  Buy   │─│   Buy    │─│ Become   │
│ stocks │ │ property │ │  self-   │
└────────┘ └────┬─────┘ │employed  │
                │       └──────────┘
                ▼
           ┌──────────┐
           │  GAIN    │
           │ CHOICE   │
           └──────────┘
```

This is the framework of this book and also of your personal financial autonomy action plan, which I hope you'll create either while you read this book or when you have finished it.

Part One: Your goals

We start with your goals. If there's no clarity on where you're trying to get to, it's impossible to know if you're even heading in the right direction, let alone making progress.

Part Two: Your cash flow

Then, we look at cash flow – income and expenses. If you spend more than you earn, no investment strategy is going to put you on the path to gaining choice. You need to be deliberate with your spending and maximise your savings. Part Two of the book explains six different money-management approaches and provides an easy-to-use tool to help you choose the one most likely to suit you.

This cash-flow stage is incredibly important. Maximising your income and aligning your spending to your goals can have an enormous impact on your autonomy and happiness. Some financial autonomy goals can be achieved solely by good money management; I've included case studies of real people who have done just that.

Importantly, this isn't about living a frugal, miserable life. Spend money on what makes you happiest, but do so with a plan, recognising that money spent on one thing can't then be spent on something else.

Parts Three to Five: The three paths

Next, we have three pathways – investing in stocks (also called shares or equities), investing in property and pursuing self-employment. After 20 years spent helping people gain choice, my observation is that everyone uses at least one of these pathways to reach success. Most people use at least two, and plenty (myself included) use a combination of all three.

The first two paths, investing in stocks and property, could be considered the most traditional ways to build financial security. They each have their pros and cons, and we'll explore those. However, they have the same destination: assets that can produce passive income, income that flows to you without you having to get out of bed.

The self-employment pathway is a bit different: this is where the idea of financial autonomy departs from the traditional idea of financial independence. Our goal is to gain choice. Now, for very many people, that choice involves how they use their time. A common financial autonomy goal, for example, is being able to be involved and engaged in children's lives when they're young, particularly until they reach secondary school. People often want to be able to do school pick-ups, help in the classroom, volunteer for the parents' association or make costumes for the ballet concert.

Speaking as a parent with two teenage boys who are close to adulthood, those kindergarten and primary-school years are fleeting and special. It's easy to turn around one day and find your children have lives of their own and that hanging out with Mum or Dad is not at the top of their 'Most desirable things to do' list. You've hopefully got 80-plus years on this planet. If you've chosen to be a parent, then you have perhaps a dozen of those years in which to influence the trajectory of another human's life and lay the foundations for a relationship with them. It's a window of opportunity not to be missed.

Self-employment may be your pathway to achieving financial autonomy, not because you aspire to be the next Bill Gates, but because you seek the flexibility that self-employment allows.

The desire to pursue a creative life could be another reason to choose self-employment as a financial autonomy pathway.

Perhaps you're a musician, for example: to really devote yourself to this pursuit, you need to get out and perform. This might require you to be out late into the night, and to tour around the country or even internationally. That's hard to make work if you're tied to a traditional nine-to-five job with four weeks of annual leave. However, if you've been able to configure a self-employment solution that covers your income needs and provides the flexibility to work remotely and when it suits you, you can chase your dream.

The Financial Autonomy workbook

Throughout this book, I've included self-assessment tools, checklists and templates to help propel you forward in developing your financial autonomy plan. If you're like me and find the idea of writing in a book akin to eating off your knife at the dinner table, download the free companion workbook, which combines all the resources in this book, from www.financialautonomy.com.au/workbook. I encourage you to download this now and print it off. That way, you can complete it as you work through this book, and you'll have a financial autonomy plan ready to move forward with at its conclusion.

Right, that's enough preamble – let's start making some progress! Here's your first self-assessment quiz. Its job is to help you identify which of the financial autonomy pathways is most likely to suit your personality and circumstances. Jump in and let's see what you learn.

Self-assessment: Financial autonomy pathways

Read each question and choose the response that feels most right for you of the three options available. If a particular question has no relevance to you (for example, the question about your boss if you're already self-employed), just skip it.

1. I have a good capacity to save on a regular basis.
   a) Some capacity to save.
   b) Yes, that's me exactly.
   c) No, my ability to save is pretty limited.

2. I'm interested in podcasts, books and blogs on marketing and entrepreneurship.
   a) Not at all.
   b) Sometimes.
   c) Yep, that's me.

3. I/We have paid off our home and now have significant surplus cash to build an investment.
   a) Yes.
   b) Not even close/I don't own a home.
   c) Not paid off yet but well on the way.

4. I've owned stocks in the past but found the volatility stressful.
   a) Yes, very much so.
   b) No. I've owned stocks and volatility is not an issue.
   c) I've never owned stocks.

5. I'm pretty 'handy' and enjoy renovation projects.
   a) That's me.
   b) A renovation project would be my worst nightmare.
   c) I can do the basics but only what I have to.

6. I've got a busy life. Any pathway I follow must require minimum time.
   a) I can always find some free time if needed.

b) Spot on.

c) No, I've got time to take on new projects that interest me.

7. I like learning and experimenting and am constantly curious.
   a) Sometimes.
   b) Often.
   c) Yes, that's me 100 per cent.

8. I need regular income from my financial autonomy pathway – ideally monthly.
   a) Definitely.
   b) Income would be good, but it doesn't need to be monthly.
   c) My needs are pretty flexible.

9. My boss is a moron; I could run this business so much more successfully.
   a) No interest at all in running a business.
   b) Not really.
   c) Totally.

10. I dislike conflict and would never want to manage staff.
    a) I'd never say 'never', but it's not a strong desire.
    b) Correct, that's me.
    c) Not at all, I like to manage people or could see myself being good at it.

11. I've always dreamed of: (You can select more than one option here.)
    a) Owning an investment property.
    b) Owning a stock portfolio.
    c) Starting my own business.

12. I enjoy my job and see myself staying put long term.
    a) Correct.
    b) Depends on the day.
    c) No.

13. My family relies on my income to meet our needs. The priority therefore is consistent and reliable income.
    a) Certainly a consideration.
    b) Definitely.
    c) Doesn't apply to me.

Which financial autonomy pathway is right for you?

Tally up how many times you have answered a), b) or c) respectively.

Your score	Interpretation
Mostly a's	If the bulk of your responses were a's, then investing in property is most likely to be a good pathway for you to explore.
Mostly b's	If the bulk of your responses were b's, take a look at investing in stocks.
Mostly c's	If c was your favourite answer, the self-employment pathway is likely to be your primary financial autonomy solution of choice.

As I mentioned earlier, most people will achieve financial autonomy through at least two pathways, so check which answers (a's, b's or c's) got the second most votes. That pathway may warrant investigation as well.

WHERE TO NOW?

I'm conscious and respectful of your time, so I encourage you to jump about this book as suits you. The hours you dedicate to digesting its contents are hours you can't spend doing something else, and I want to ensure you get full value for the investment that you make. I want to deliver you results – get you on the path to gaining choice. So, if your pathway is likely to be property and self-employment, feel free to skip the chapters on investing in stocks. You might even want to read the self-employment section first, then the stocks section. Absolutely fine by me. This isn't *Lord of the Rings* – you don't need to read the book chapter by chapter in order to follow the story. There are no rules here.

Before you jump into Parts Three, Four and Five to focus on your financial autonomy pathways, however, I do urge you to read Part One and the chapter 'Goal-setting with purpose'. Without a clear goal, you'll be running around like the classic chicken with its head cut off. I also encourage you to digest Part Two, 'Cash flow'. Investing in stocks and property requires that you use your savings to purchase these assets – logically, the more savings you have, the more rapidly you can do this. If self-employment is your financial autonomy pathway of choice, managing your cash flow may still be an important precursor, as you will likely need some initial capital investment, and perhaps a runway to give the venture time to succeed.

Congratulations on embracing the idea of financial autonomy. Let's get started building your personal roadmap to gaining the choice in life that you deserve!

PART ONE
DEFINE SUCCESS

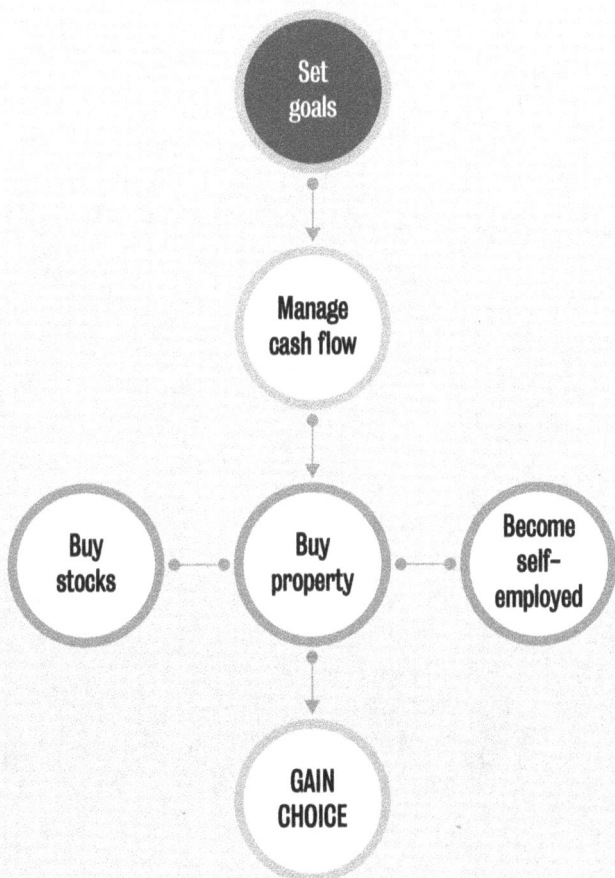

1

GOAL-SETTING WITH PURPOSE

Step 1 on your financial autonomy journey is to set your goals. Goal-setting is an essential foundational step because it defines the direction you are heading, and what success looks like.

However, setting the goal is not enough in isolation. Every sporting team starts the season with the goal of being number one at the end of the season, but most don't succeed. The goal, while essential, is just the first step – you also need a strategy and you need to take action. The later chapters in this book are intended to help you do just that.

Goal-setting has another benefit, too: it increases your happiness. I've thought about and written a lot on happiness, because when you boil it down, that's the core aim. Whether your goal is to send your kids to a private school, visit Antarctica, or own a Porsche 911, what you're really chasing is happiness.

There are many definitions of happiness, but this is the one that has resonated most with me over the years:

Happiness is making progress towards a worthwhile goal.

I find this to be a really interesting insight. Happiness isn't some fleeting thing that only occurs when you reach your goal. Rather, it's something you experience as you make progress.

Last summer, I had a goal of completing the Lorne Pier to Pub ocean-swimming race. I was successful in achieving that goal, and the day itself was wonderful, but the training process was also terrific. In order to get there, I joined a swimming group and trained several times a week. I met some great people, making new friends as we went along. I also got a huge amount of satisfaction from the improvement I made as the training progressed – being able to cover distances that a month or two earlier had felt well out of reach. Happiness is making progress towards a worthwhile goal.

If you're willing to embrace this definition of happiness, then:

1. It's really worthwhile setting some goals.
2. There's lots of potential happiness for you to enjoy on your journey to achieve those goals.

WHAT'S YOUR 'WHY'?

Before we get into laying down your financial autonomy goals, let's take a step back for a moment. Author and speaker Simon Sinek wrote the book *Start With Why* in 2009 and has delivered some great TED Talks on this idea that you might want to take a look at. When it comes to setting your goals, taking a few moments to first reflect on your 'why' is likely to be time well spent. The key is to dig down multiple layers. Here's a personal example of mine that I completed when working on my business plan. My goal is to grow my business:

- Why? To get business revenue growing.
- Why? To increase profit.
- Why? For financial security and lifestyle.
- Why else? To be able to reduce reliance on me by building a team.
- Why? For lifestyle (travel) and increased business value (not being owner-centric).
- Why else? With a larger team, I can focus on doing the bits I like doing and hand off other things to staff.

Hopefully you can see here that by not stopping at the first answer, by asking why again and again, I was able to get at what I was really trying to achieve.

Executing a plan to achieve a particular goal rarely happens without any setbacks or things out of left field that you hadn't considered. Adaptation is therefore an essential requirement in achieving success. In start-up land, they call it a 'pivot'. The risk, when faced with the need to make changes, is knowing which path is the right path. That's where being clear on your 'why' is so crucial. Your 'why' is your magnetic north. It guides you towards progress through the normal twists and turns of life.

Let's consider an example. Say that you want to move to self-employment so as to have the flexibility to work around your kids' school drop-offs and getting them to their after-school activities. You use your skills as a compliance manager, built up over ten years of employment, and start your own one-person business, providing compliance services for three medium-sized businesses, mainly from your home office with occasional site visits as needed. You're working around 20 hours per week. You'd like a few more hours, ideally about 30 in total, but all things considered, you're in a good place.

One of your clients buys another business, and as a result roughly doubles in size. They approach you about working one day per week on site at the new business to help with the integration. They'd require you to be in the office from 8.30 a.m. until 5 p.m. and the office is 30 minutes' drive from home.

Now, without a clear 'why', this opportunity would seem to be a good one. You wanted more hours – well, here they are. But because you have a clear 'why', you can consider whether in fact this opportunity is one you should be taking. It doesn't provide flexibility, and the hours plus the commute don't allow you to do the things with your children that were the whole reason for moving to self-employment in the first place.

Knowing your 'why' makes your decision process easier.

EFFECTIVE GOAL-SETTING

With clarity on your 'why', let's move onto setting your goals. The number-one mistake people make when setting goals is not being specific enough. They create vague goals like, 'I want to pay off the mortgage'. Well, sure, anyone with a mortgage does. However, a vague goal like that doesn't give you much scope to develop a plan to achieve it, or enable you to set milestones, another essential step in successful goal-setting. A more useful goal would be, 'I want the mortgage to be under $100,000 by the time I'm 40, and paid off entirely by the time I reach 45'.

A popular framework when it comes to goal-setting that you've quite likely come across before is SMART, an acronym for:

- specific
- measurable
- actionable
- realistic
- time bound.

Here's an example of applying the SMART methodology to your goals.

Let's say you had a goal to own a house near the beach one day. It's somewhere that perhaps you would retire to later in life, but you'd like it to be a holiday house until then: just somewhere you and your family can escape to and spend quality time together. So the first step is to be 'specific'. Where do you want to have the beach house? How many rooms would it need to have? Your goal might then become, 'I want to own a house near the beach, in the Inverloch region of Victoria, that has at least four bedrooms and two bathrooms'.

The next step is to make your goal 'measurable'. Do a little bit of internet research and determine what the house is likely to cost. Let's say you determine that a suitable property is likely to cost around $400,000.

On to 'actionable' and 'realistic'. Given your current financial position and income, is there a genuine likelihood that you can achieve this goal? You may not know the exact path, but you should have a sense of whether it's possible, then finally 'time bound' – that might be 'By the time I'm 50'.

So, your original goal was to own a house near the beach one day. Your goal, re-expressed as a SMART goal, becomes, 'By the time I'm 50, I want to own a house near the beach in the Inverloch region, which has at least four bedrooms and two bathrooms, and I expect to need to spend around $400,000'. Your goal has gone from a 'one day, maybe' proposition, to something that is quantified and really specific. With this nailed down, you can now work on a plan to get you there – whereas before, how would you know if you were making progress?

Goal categories

One more thing to consider, before you put this book down for a few minutes and write down your goals: there are different categories of goals. Sure, this book has the word 'financial' in the title, but that doesn't mean all of your goals should be about money. Here are the goal categories I like to consider:

- experiences
- things
- relationships
- altruism.

I'm not saying you need to have a goal in each category: rather, just consider each category and reflect on whether happiness lies there for you. Here are a few examples to help your thinking:

- **Experiences**
  Hike the Inca Trail to Machu Picchu, take the kids to Disneyland, learn a new language, take six months to travel around the country, learn to surf, attend the Glastonbury Festival in the UK.

- **Things**

  Pay off the mortgage, upgrade to a larger/better house, buy the sports car of your teenage dreams, renovate the kitchen, get a second home near the beach or in the country.

- **Relationships**

  Have the time to fully participate in your children's lives, take care of your elderly parents, ensure your partner knows you appreciate them.

- **Altruism**

  Volunteer for a local community organisation, make regular donations to a cause of significance to you, help out family members in need.

Include your partner

If you have a partner, it's essential that you include them in your financial autonomy journey, especially in this goal-setting phase. Psychotherapist Dr Barton Goldsmith goes so far as to say, 'Goals are a relationship necessity' (and wrote an article with this name for *Psychology Today* back in 2010).

If the choice in life that you're seeking involves a major change, like a new career or moving to self-employment, it's possible your partner might be reluctant. Things are comfortable now: why take the risk? I'm not a relationship counsellor, but an approach could be to paint a picture of what success looks like. For example, if your goal is to cut back to three days per week of paid employment, you could talk about the extra family time that will allow, or the reduction in stress levels in the household.

If your partner does have concerns, acknowledge them, and then try and find solutions together. There may be value in getting some financial modelling done so you can really see how things will look in a money sense if you pursue this goal.

I met a great couple recently, Tim and Sarah, who were about to have their first child. They wanted to know if it would be possible for Tim to quit his job and become a tennis coach. He didn't need to do this straight away, but wanted it to happen sometime in the next ten years. We were able to do the financial modelling for them and show a couple of ways for him to achieve this goal. It was a great way for the two of them to understand what was possible, and also what the costs were – in this case, working longer before retirement.

Two people working together on a common set of goals can accomplish far more than two individuals with separate agendas.

Gaining choice is more important than ever

In my lifetime, we've witnessed the internet rise from nothingness to omnipresence, with the world's knowledge in our pocket.

If you had a *Doctor Who*–style time machine, you could pick someone up in 1500 AD, drop them off 200 years later and, while they'd undoubtedly notice some changes, they'd be able to get on with life just fine after a little adjustment. Pick someone up from 1820 and drop them into today's world, though, and you'd see their head explode – planes, cars, phones, television, credit cards, and the enormous change in women's roles in our society would be a huge shift from their own time.

Not only is change a constant, change is accelerating. Tim Urban, in his great article 'The AI revolution: the road to super-intelligence', highlighted the link between Moore's law (the concept that computing power doubles roughly every two years) and the advancement of artificial intelligence. AI today isn't close to being as smart as a human, simply because we don't have computers able to process information as quickly as our brains can. However, applying Moore's law to today's computing power, we'll have computers with human-like processing speed in 20 to 30 years.

Change, then, is not slowing down. In fact, acceleration of AI capabilities could massively up-end our current employment world – trucks that drive themselves, for example, will put current truck drivers and couriers out of work. Accountants, medical specialists, engineers, and (heaven forbid) even financial planners may well be replaced by computers that are able to access every piece of knowledge available and provide better solutions than we ever could have.

However, human history has shown that we adapt. When the industrial revolution began, many were fearful that the cotton weavers and blacksmiths would be put out of work, with no new opportunities to go to. Of course, instead, new opportunities grew enormously – and so too will they for us in the future. But we need to be able to embrace them. Retraining mid working life will become more and more important (and perhaps lead to a more interesting life, too), but it's tough to retrain when you're buckling under the strain of debt and mounting bills.

Building your financial strength, your resiliency, has never been more important than it is today. The future will be wonderful, but you need to ensure you're in the driver's seat.

ACTION TIME

Okay, it's time for you to take some action. In your workbook or on a sheet of paper, write down some goals that will see you gain choice in life. Start with a brain dump of ideas, then refine and consolidate them. Keep in mind the importance of detail.

Prioritisation

Hopefully, you now have several goals that you want to achieve in your pursuit of gaining choice. To move forward and develop an actionable plan, it's essential that you prioritise these goals, as often it's not possible to focus on two goals simultaneously. For instance, if one of your goals is to pay off your mortgage, and another is a family trip to Disneyland, money devoted to one denies you the other goal.

Now, you could simply look at your list of goals and rank them from one down, but I've got a more robust system for you. I learned the following technique several years back: I've found it enormously helpful in developing a plan for achievement of my goals, and I use it with clients all the time. Let me take you through an example.

Let's say that your goals are as follows:

- Pay off my $375,000 mortgage by the time I turn 45.
- Take a family holiday to Disneyland in two years' time when my oldest child is twelve.
- Build a nest egg to enable a comfortable retirement at age 60 on an income of at least $75,000 per year.
- Renovate the kitchen and bathroom next year, with a budget of $40,000.

These four objectives were recorded in the order they came out of your head, and so it would be tempting to assume they automatically reflect your priorities. My experience is that this is rarely the case.

Here's how to find the true priority:

- Ask yourself: if you were only given a choice between the first or second objective – mortgage or Disneyland – which would you choose? You have to pick one, but you can't pick both. Whatever your answer is, put a tick next to that one.

- Next, look at the first and third objectives. If you could only choose one, would it be mortgage or nest egg?

- How about mortgage or kitchen?

- Now compare the second and third objectives, then the second and fourth, and finally the third and fourth.

At the end of this process, you should have compared each objective head to head and have come out with something that looks like this:

✓ Pay off my $375,000 mortgage by the time I turn 45.

✓✓ Take a family holiday to Disneyland in two years' time when my oldest child is twelve.

Build a nest egg to enable a comfortable retirement at age 60 on an income of at least $75,000 per year.

✓✓✓ Renovate the kitchen and bathroom next year, with a budget of $40,000.

The kitchen got three votes, Disneyland two, and the mortgage only one, despite it being the first goal that came to mind. This is the sort of outcome I see pretty much every time I go through this exercise with people.

Now you can say the order of priority for your objectives is:

1. Renovate the kitchen and bathroom next year, with a budget of $40,000.

2. Take a family holiday to Disneyland in two years' time when my oldest child is twelve.

3. Pay off my $375,000 mortgage by the time I turn 45.

4. Build a nest egg to enable a comfortable retirement at age 60 on an income of at least $75,000 per year.

Paying off the mortgage is important, but that kitchen really needs to get done, and the kids are only going to be at an age to enjoy Disneyland for a short window. It would be great to focus on building retirement savings but, for now, normal employer contributions to super will have to suffice.

Now you not only have good-quality goals, you also have them prioritised accurately.

WHERE ARE YOU NOW?

Ever decided it was time to lose some weight? Perhaps it was a New Year's resolution, or spurred by an upcoming seaside holiday. After a bit of procrastination (should you do more exercise, eat less food, or a bit of both?), the first thing you do is weigh yourself.

Why? Well, how will you know if your hard work is getting results unless you know your starting point? Most important of all, as you shed the weight, your progress provides the fuel for you to keep going.

Shortly, you'll complete the first portion of your financial autonomy action plan. Before you do that, though, it's helpful to gain clarity on where you currently sit financially.

To understand this, you need to construct your personal balance sheet and determine your net asset position. It's a simple process that will take you five to ten minutes at most. Simply fill in the numbers in the following table, or in your workbook or on a sheet of paper. Leave blank any areas that don't apply to you, and add any items that aren't listed.

Assets	$	Liabilities	$
Home		Mortgage	
Car(s)		Car loan(s)	
Cash in bank (including any offset accounts)		Other loans	
Investments		Credit card(s)	
Retirement savings		Tax debt	
TOTAL		**TOTAL**	

Here's a worked example for you.

Assets	$	Liabilities	$
Home	950,000	Mortgage	460,000
Cars	35,000	Car loan	12,500
Cash in bank (including offset account)	83,500	Other loans	
Investments	4,500	Credit card(s)	
		Tax debt	
TOTAL	1,073,000	**TOTAL**	472,500
NET ASSET POSITION			600,500

Monitoring your net asset position (sometimes referred to as your 'net wealth' or 'net worth') can be a very useful way to monitor progress. I calculate my family's at least once a year.

It's useful to have this done before you embark on your financial autonomy journey, because while your 'why' and your goals are essential so that you know where's north on your compass, navigation is impossible if you don't know where you are now. As an example, if I had the goals listed in the previous exercise, but also owed $20,000 on a credit card, then irrespective of my desire to achieve these goals, they'd all need to be placed on hold while I focused on clearing that card.

PREREQUISITES

You'll flesh things out more when you get to the relevant chapters, but it's appropriate at this goal-setting stage to consider whether your goals have any prerequisites. For instance, if the choice you want to gain is to do with time flexibility, self-employment may be the pathway for you. What are the prerequisites for this? Do you need a new laptop from which to run your empire, or the services of a good accountant to ensure that you pay all the taxes you're required to? Perhaps you need to learn some new skills like online marketing? For the objectives we looked at earlier, the goal of renovating the kitchen and bathroom will require design work to be done and builders to be engaged.

These prerequisites can provide milestones for you to track, and milestones are an incredibly useful way to maintain momentum on your financial autonomy journey.

ACTION PLAN TIME

Throughout this book, you'll work towards building your action plan: now's the time to make a start! Grab a sheet of paper and write four headings across the top (if you have downloaded the workbook, you can use that):

Financial autonomy goal	Success is	Financial autonomy pathway and strategy	Actions I will take during the next 3 months

Enter the top three goals that you identified through the prioritisation exercise in the left-most column. Next, go to the second column and complete the 'Success is' section – both long term and in three months. The three-month success points – milestones – can pick up those prerequisites you identified a few moments ago.

Overleaf is a completed plan, so you can get a feel for it. (We'll look at the 'Financial autonomy pathway and strategy' column later in the book, of course.)

My financial autonomy action plan

Financial autonomy goal	Success is
Renovate the kitchen and bathroom next year, with a budget of $40,000.	**Long term:** Renovation done. **In 3 months' time:** Our offset account balance is ~$29,000.
Take a family holiday to Disneyland in two years' time when my oldest child is twelve.	**Long term:** Get to Disneyland. **In 3 months' time:** Goal is quantified.
Pay off my $375,000 mortgage by the time I turn 45.	**Long term:** Mortgage is repaid. **In 3 months' time:** Loan is approved and money available to invest.
Pay off my $375,000 mortgage by the time I turn 45.	**Long term:** Mortgage is repaid. **In 3 months' time:** Loan balance is lower than it is today.
Build a nest egg to enable a comfortable retirement at age 60 on an income of at least $75,000 per year.	**Long term:** Comfortable retirement. **In 3 months' time:** Balance growth.
Build a nest egg to enable a comfortable retirement at age 60 on an income of at least $75,000 per year.	**Long term:** A debt-free investment property to provide additional options in retirement. **In 3 months' time:** N/A

Financial autonomy pathway and strategy	Actions I will take during the next 3 months
• Pathway – Cash-flow management. • Add $1,200 per month to our offset account (current balance ~$26,000).	Set up automatic transfer from living account for $600 each payday across to offset account.
• Pathway – Cash-flow management. • Save for this once kitchen renovations are done.	Determine what this trip will cost and how much we need to save each month.
• Pathway 1 – Stocks. • Use equity in home to buy a $200k stock portfolio. Use dividends to pay down home loan. Capital growth upon selldown to make lump sum repayment.	Speak with my mortgage broker and get loan facility in place.
• Pathway 2 – Cash flow. • Pay $200 per month over required minimum. • Use offset accounts for all savings. • Pay annual bonuses and tax returns off loan as lump sum repayments.	Continue with current setting.
• Pathway 1 – Stocks (via superannuation). • Employer contributions only until mortgage is repaid, then maximise. • Use the aggressive investment option.	None
• Pathway 2 – Property. • In 5 years, look to use equity in our home to fund deposit on an investment property.	None

Before we move onto the next chapter, let's summarise what we've covered here in 'Goal-setting with purpose':

- Be clear on your 'why'. Dig several layers deep to get to your true answer.

- Do a brain dump of all the goals you can think of.

- Consolidate these initial thoughts into several specific goals – think about the SMART acronym.

- Be sure to include your partner if you have one.

- Complete the prioritisation exercise – the initial order in which your goals flow from your brain is unlikely to reflect your true priorities.

- Complete your personal balance sheet to be clear on where you are now – your net asset position, your starting point.

- Identify any prerequisites to your goals.

- Make a start on your financial autonomy action plan.

Phew! We've covered a lot in chapter 1 – they are important foundations, though, that will set you up for success. Congratulations on your progress! Let's now move onto Part Two, 'Cash flow' – perhaps the number-one prerequisite when it comes to achieving financial autonomy.

PART TWO
CASH FLOW

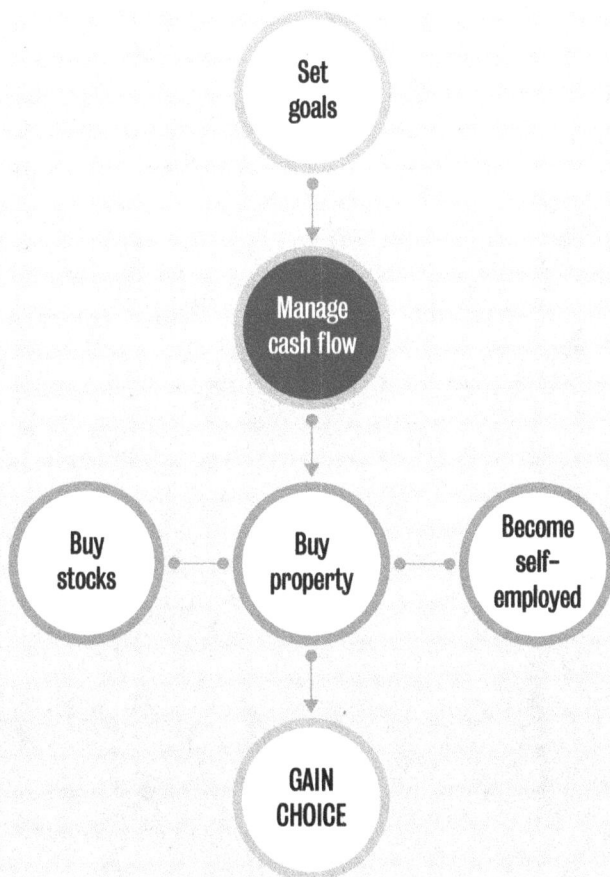

```
        ┌──────────┐
        │   Set    │
        │  goals   │
        └────┬─────┘
             │
        ┌────▼─────┐
        │  Manage  │
        │cash flow │
        └────┬─────┘
             │
┌────────┐  ┌────────┐  ┌────────┐
│  Buy   │──│  Buy   │──│ Become │
│ stocks │  │property│  │ self-  │
└────────┘  └───┬────┘  │employed│
                │       └────────┘
            ┌───▼────┐
            │  GAIN  │
            │ CHOICE │
            └────────┘
```

2

CASH-FLOW MASTERY

If you're spending more than you're earning, then you have no hope of building wealth and long-term financial security. Most importantly, you have no hope of achieving financial autonomy and gaining choice.

This chapter is titled 'Cash-flow' – 'cash flow' is money coming in and money going out. Flowing. Very deliberately, this chapter is not called 'Budgeting'. Here's why:

- Most people associate the word 'budgeting' with negativity and less happiness.

- Many people think that having a budget means tracking every dollar that they spend, sending themselves and those around them to the lunatic asylum.

- Budgeting tends to imply it's all about the spending, and while conscious and deliberate spending is important,

I prefer to think about 'cash flow' because it includes the other half of the equation – income.

Mastering cash flow is a foundation step in getting onto the pathway of financial success. In fact, even though this book focuses on the three pathways – investing in stocks, investing in property and becoming self-employed – some choices can be achieved through cash-flow strategies alone. If your expenses are low enough, then your income needs can more easily be met, immediately providing you with greater choice in life even before you embark on any of the pathways.

Financial autonomy in action: Minimising expenses to gain choice

In episode 104 of the Financial Autonomy podcast, I chatted with Melbourne-based author Annie Raser-Roland, whose beautifully written book *The Art of Frugal Hedonism* is a fantastic read. In our discussion, Annie shared that she now does only one day of traditional paid work per week, with book royalties, occasional speaking fees and investment income combining to generate enough money to not only meet her needs but also enable her to save. She's able to travel – she has a particular passion for long hiking trips – and lives a fun and happy life, with enormous time flexibility. She shared that, if the weather is lovely, she'll give herself the day or afternoon off from writing and go visit friends or read a book by a local river.

In Annie's case, she's solved her cash-flow needs by cutting back on expenses quite severely. Low living costs mean she doesn't need a huge income, and with no need to generate a large wage, she has the time to put her energy into the things she is passionate about: writing and friends. Annie has certainly been successful in gaining choice, and all by putting considerable effort into developing a cash-flow strategy that works for her.

As an aside, during our chat we touched on retirement. Annie pointed to David Attenborough as her model – so long as you can do stuff you love, just keeping doing it. She also observed that her current life enables her to travel and enjoy life to the full, so how would retirement in the traditional sense make her happier or more fulfilled?

I love and fully endorse this thinking. It also provides a little insight into another enabler of choice. The shorter the period of life that you expect to produce no income and live entirely off your investments, the less you need to focus on building up retirement savings. Put another way, someone planning on a 50-year working life can afford to earn less each year than someone targeting only a 30-year working life. And if you can earn less, then you can work less, gaining the time to do what makes you happy. This is gaining choice in full bloom.

I wouldn't personally want to cut my expenses down to Annie's level, and frugal living at the extreme end isn't for most people. However, thinking about how you spend your money is massively worthwhile, as is recognising that higher living costs require higher income to keep the ship sailing.

Episode 55 of my podcast, about Tim's successful career change, provided another example of using cash-flow strategies to gain choice. Let's explore this next.

Financial autonomy in action: Rethinking the budget to enable a career change

Tim graduated from university with a science degree, but wasn't able to find work in that field and so started working at a bank. It was never intended to be his forever career, but a family came along, and promotions, and before he knew it, he'd been at the bank 19 years.

Teaching was a career that had been on his mind since his university days. However, he'd pushed the idea of a career change out of his head for a long time, as the responsibilities of raising three children with his wife Mary-Anne took priority. Sure, his heart hadn't been in banking for some time, but a shift to teaching would mean doing a master's degree. Two years of study. Two years of no income. Making that work financially was a major hurdle.

Tim and Mary-Anne were working on a plan whereby she would increase her hours to earn extra income and that, combined with some cuts in the discretionary portion of the family budget, would make the master's a possibility. Then Tim got offered a redundancy package: that injection of cash meant it was game on.

They developed a cash-flow plan. They worked out their basic costs – food, housing, bills, health care and school fees – and determined how to pay for these through a combination of Mary-Anne's income and a drip-feed of Tim's redundancy package. They were fortunate in that Tim got six months' notice of the redundancy, so they were able to test the plan for three months, fine-tuning as they went along.

Returning to school at 45 was not without its challenges; however, Tim persevered, and I'm pleased to report he is now a well-loved and respected primary-school teacher. In fact, the whole thing went so well that once Tim was settled, Mary-Anne decided she wanted to join the career-change party and left the defence department to become a police officer. Clearly this household knows how to make career changes!

Tim and Mary-Anne's experience illustrates the power of managing your cash flow to gain choice. It also highlights that gaining choice can lead to happier lives.

When it comes to managing your day-to-day spending, Ramit Sethi puts it really well in his book *I Will Teach You to Be Rich*. He writes, 'spend extravagantly on the things you love as long as you cut costs mercilessly on the things you don't'. Maybe travel is the thing you love. Perhaps it's eating out. Maybe it's exotic cocktails on a Friday night. Or perhaps it's a Porsche!

If it gives you enormous joy, go for it, but recognise that you can't do everything. Pick one or two things, throw yourself into them and have a blast. But if it's, say, the Porsche that gets you excited, don't then head off on an expensive holiday. Similarly, if you've planned to do a six-week trek in the Andes later in the year, be prepared to say no when a friend suggests you catch up for brunch on the weekend at a local café. (Perhaps suggest going for a walk together instead – I'm not advocating ditching your friends!) The point is, be conscious of how you spend your money.

A related point is, once you've worked out a cash-flow strategy and you've achieved your milestones, you shouldn't feel bad or guilty about spending your money on the things you've chosen. The goal is not to end up the richest person in the cemetery! What you're trying to achieve is greater happiness through a more deliberate and structured plan to manage your money.

YOUR SAVINGS RATE

In chapter 3, we'll run through six different cash-flow strategies that you could adopt. Before you nail down your strategy, though, you might want to park the concept of your savings rate in your brain. Your savings rate is simply the percentage of your after-tax income that you save. Here's an example to illustrate:

After-tax income per month	$8,000
Savings per month:	
additional mortgage payments above minimum required	$1,000
to holiday account	$300
to general savings	$300
Total savings per month	$1,600

Savings rate = 1,600 ÷ 8,000 = 20%

I've found monitoring my savings rate useful in a couple of ways. First, I make it a personal challenge to see how high I can get the rate before our lifestyle is impacted. The highest I've managed is 55 per cent, though it wasn't sustainable. Second, it's a high-level tracking tool in the same category as your net asset position, which was discussed in chapter 1. It's a bit like a blood-pressure check – a good piece of baseline information on your financial health. Also, if it's something that you track over time, a change, especially downwards, can act as the canary in the coal mine and get you checking what has altered in your cash-flow strategy and deciding whether any changes are necessary.

Something I like about the savings rate is that it picks up both expenses and income, and you can improve your savings rate via increasing your income, while keeping your expenses exactly the same. As mentioned earlier, it's essential to be conscious and deliberate with your spending, but I don't advocate extreme, penny-pinching frugality as the route to a happy life.

Improving your savings rate can have a big impact over time. The following chart compares two rates – 20 per cent and 30 per cent. In both instances, monthly income is $8,000 and it's assumed that your savings will earn 5 per cent per year. (Clearly this is not a 'cash in the bank' earning rate: I'm assuming use of low- to medium-risk investments.) The axis across the bottom is the number of months; I've run it out over ten years or 120 months.

Over this time period, having your savings rate at the higher 30 per cent results in an additional $124,743 in savings, with that differential growing further as time goes on.

Savings rate comparison

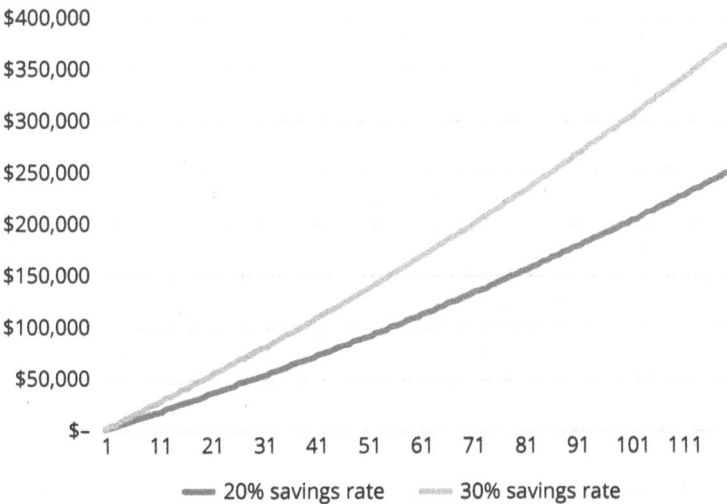

Legend: 20% savings rate, 30% savings rate

Take a moment right now to determine your current savings rate using the following table, or by completing it in your workbook.

Don't worry about being precise down to the last dollar: you can refine it later if you find it useful.

Monthly savings	$
Extra mortgage payments	
Cash into savings accounts	
Additions to investment portfolios	
Non-compulsory retirement savings	
Children's education savings	
Other	
TOTAL MONTHLY SAVINGS	
Monthly after-tax income	
Savings rate (divide total savings by after-tax income)	

If you feel the inclination, you could make your savings rate calculation quite nuanced. You could, for instance, include the principal portion of any loan repayments, if the asset could be expected to increase in value – so, home loan yes, car loan no. You could also include compulsory or employer retirement savings. The thing to consider, though, is that except when you're trying to compare your rate with someone else's, these tweaks really don't matter much. You're trying to track change over time: consistency is therefore the priority. My view is, keep it simple!

YOUR INCOME

As I explained earlier, I've called this section 'Cash flow' rather than 'Budgeting' because success involves focusing not only on spending, but also on income. Here's how I think of the difference, with budgeting just one part of your overall cash-flow strategy:

**CASH-FLOW
STRATEGY**

Budgeting

We all have basic needs that cost money, but no matter how rich you are, spending more money on toilet paper or breakfast cereal won't make you any happier. So your expenses will always have a lower cap – the basics – and a slightly vague upper cap, where you've got everything that you need covered. Your income, however, can go from zero to lots and lots, depending on your skill set, opportunities and determination.

Your income can rise for a variety of reasons, including:

- getting a promotion to a role with more responsibilities and higher pay

- moving to a new employer who values your skills more

- highlighting to your current employer the value you deliver to the business and negotiating a raise

- starting a side hustle

- generating income from passive investments like stocks and property

- moving to self-employment and 'cutting out the middle man' so that more of the value you create through your work passes through to you

- undertaking training to increase your skills and consequent value to employers.

So, when you think through your cash-flow strategy and how you can maximise your savings to accelerate your journey to financial autonomy, don't fall into the trap of focusing only on cutting expenses. Recognise that a vital piece of the puzzle may be to increase your income.

Having said that, your expenses are certainly the other piece of the puzzle. Let's explore this now.

DO I REALLY WANT TO SPEND MONEY ON THAT?

Let's say your financial autonomy goal is to retire early so that you can devote your time to supporting a non-profit community organisation that you have a strong affinity with. In order to make this a reality, you need to ascertain how much money you need to live. Is it $30,000 per year or $80,000 per year? It won't come as a shock to you that the higher the income you require, the more savings you'll need to accumulate. You might be surprised, however, by the degree of the impact. Here are some numbers to illustrate:

- If you wanted to build up a portfolio of investments that would generate $30,000 per year for you to live off, rising with inflation, and with a high level of confidence that it won't run out in your lifetime, you'd need investments worth around $750,000.

- If, instead of $30,000, you needed $40,000 per year, you'd need investments worth $1 million. So, to have just an extra $10,000 per year, you need to save an extra $250,000. (Note that I haven't allowed for tax here, this is just a really simple illustration.)

- To flip that, if you could reduce your living expenses by $10,000 per year, then the amount you'd need to save to be financially independent and retire early would reduce by $250,000. How much sooner would that mean you could escape your current employment captivity?

- If $80,000 per year was the amount needed to meet your living costs, the capital required is $2 million.

You may have heard of the book *The Millionaire Next Door*. The two authors, Thomas Stanley and William Danko, studied households whose net assets exceeded $1 million. One really interesting finding was that millionaire households were disproportionately clustered in blue-collar and middle-class suburbs, and not in the higher income, white-collar, more affluent suburbs that you would assume. Digging into why this was the case, the authors found that the higher-income-earners spent more on luxury items and status symbols, often funded with debt, and tended to neglect savings and investment. This may have been due to confidence that their income-earning capacity would continue to support them in future, but more likely it was because their budgets incorporated spending associated with maintaining a certain social status.

The lesson from *The Millionaire Next Door* would seem to be, don't lease the expensive car, don't buy the $1,000 handbag or the $300 pair of jeans. Avoid the status symbols and the debts often linked to them. A fulfilling life means different things to different people, but if you want to be financially independent and have choice in life, then you need to jettison the need to keep up with the Joneses.

CREDIT CARDS

If you brought together 1,000 people in serious financial difficulty, 999 of them would have credit-card debt – and the one who didn't no doubt applied for a card but had such a bad credit rating that the credit-card issuers wouldn't touch them. Credit cards are the gateway drug to spending more than you earn and getting yourself into financial difficulty.

But here's the thing – they are also very useful. Because of their potential for disaster, many money experts will advocate not having credit cards, but I'm not in that camp. My wife and I have a credit card. Indeed, I have a second card for my business. Given the increasingly common practice of shopping online, and of cashless transactions even in physical stores, I believe credit cards have a place in most people's financial lives. They are invaluable when travelling overseas, and some have rewards programs that can be quite helpful – ours provides free travel insurance when you pay for your airline tickets with the card, which has saved us hundreds if not thousands of dollars over the years. You just need to pay your cards off, and you need to avoid overspending.

Many credit cards have an interest-free period, so provided you pay the balance off by the required date, you pay no interest. The credit-card issuer still makes money by charging shop owners a fee, and likely by charging you an annual fee too – so you're not 'gaming the system' by paying your card off when it's due, you're just playing within the rules.

The issue, then, is being able to pay off your credit card when it's due, and that circles back to the biggest potential problem with credit cards: their capacity to enable overspending. Here are my thoughts on how you can avoid this pitfall:

- **When you spend on your card, clear it straight away**
  This is the approach my wife and I use with the grocery shopping. We pay with the credit card to get the reward points, but as soon as we exit the supermarket, we transfer the money from our 'living' bank account to the credit card using the banking app on our mobile phones. There's no

need to wait for the credit-card bill to come in to make a payment: you can make a payment at any time.

The benefit of this approach is that our budget strategy relies on us paying for all our day-to-day needs from the 'living' account, which gets replenished each fortnight. As the account runs down, we see that we need to tighten the belt to ensure we don't run out until next payday. Paying off the credit card as soon as it is used, rather than waiting for the monthly statement, ensures that this approach works and prevents overspending. (If overspending on credit cards is a problem for you, choose a budget strategy from chapter 3 that's suited to reining that in. Zero-based budgeting is likely to be best, or the 'track your spending' approach.)

- **Have savings**
  Sometimes overspending isn't really due to financial ill-discipline – it's just that your spending needs are lumpy. Christmas-time is often expensive, for example, as you buy gifts and, for those in the Southern Hemisphere, have your summer break. It's easy to rack up some credit-card debt during this time.

  The solution is to plan for the fact that this is an expensive time, and build up savings during the year so you have the money to pay your debt off. Also, don't get a huge credit-card limit. For most people, a $5,000 limit is enough – $10,000 maximum. More than that and you're just asking to get into a credit-card debt spiral.

Bottom line, credit cards can get people into financial difficulty, but you needn't suffer that fate. Most people manage their credit cards just fine, and you can too, especially if you adopt one of the six cash-flow management strategies explained in the next chapter.

3

SIX STRATEGIES TO MAXIMISE YOUR SAVINGS

I want to get you saving. When you have a savings regime, you build wealth and, in so doing, gain choice. There are plenty of gurus out there telling you that they have THE solution to get your money sorted. If there truly were one 'best of the best' way that worked for everyone, though, then why haven't we all adopted it, and why aren't we all in our financial happy place?

Here's the truth: beyond the fundamental requirement to spend less than you earn, there is no single money-management approach that works for all people, all of time. So, in this chapter I'm not presenting you with one single money management system, as would be the norm for books of this genre. Instead, I'm providing six strategies, each quite different and likely to suit different people:

1. the 50/20/30 method

2. the bucket strategy

3. the reverse budget

4. the big-cut strategy

5. the 'track your spending' approach

6. zero-based budgeting.

Nobody's perfect when it comes to money management, but having some sort of system is infinitely better than no system at all. Don't let the quest for perfection stop you from achieving huge progress on your financial autonomy goals – make a start, have a go, adapt, evolve and discard as necessary.

The descriptions for each strategy aren't long, so you might want to have a read of each and decide from there which you want to embrace. For those who are in more of a hurry, though, I've provided the self-assessment tool following, which is also in your workbook. Respond to its ten statements to find out which strategy is most likely to deliver success for you; there's even a 'Plan B' if the first recommendation doesn't resonate.

Online mini-course

The material in this section is derived from a mini-course I developed called 'Cash Flow Mastery'. It's a series of fourteen videos going for five to ten minutes each. If you'd like more details, go to www.financialautonomy.com.au/cashflow.

Self-assessment: Cash-flow management

1. I'm a detail-oriented person – I like precise answers.
   a) That's me.
   b) Somewhat.
   c) That's definitely not me.

2. My main goal is to pay off debt as quickly as possible.
   a) Definitely.
   b) Somewhat.
   c) Not at all.

3. I like to focus on the big picture.
   a) Nope.
   b) Sometimes.
   c) That's me.

4. I'm time-poor.
   a) Not really.
   b) Often.
   c) Always.

5. I'm great with a spreadsheet.
   a) Expert.
   b) Capable.
   c) What's a spreadsheet?

6. I've got a pretty good handle on where my money goes each month.
   a) Nope.
   b) In most cases.
   c) Definitely.

7. I've been pretty good at saving in the past.
   a) Never.
   b) Somewhat.
   c) Yes.

8. I'm comfortable talking about money with my partner/friends.
   a) Not at all.
   b) Reasonably comfortable.
   c) Yep.

9. I clear my credit card every month.
   a) I wish!
   b) Yes.
   c) I don't have a credit card.

10. I'm really fired up and driven to retire as soon as possible.
    a) That's me.
    b) Somewhat.
    c) Not my goal.

Which budget strategy is right for you?

Add up how many times you answered a), b) and c) respectively, and then calculate your score. Every a) answer is worth 3 points, every b) answer is worth 2 points and every c) answer is worth 1 point.

Your score	Recommended strategy	Plan B strategy
14–15	The big cut	50/20/30
16–18	50/20/30	Bucket or reverse budget
19–22	Bucket or reverse budget	Bucket or reverse budget
23–26	Track your spending	Bucket
27–30	Zero-based	Track your spending

THE 50/20/30 METHOD

The 50/20/30 method is a good, easy strategy to implement that doesn't require you to monitor every dollar you spend. You can have it up and running in five minutes. With this approach, you divide up your after-tax income as follows:

- 50 per cent to spend on must-haves (needs)
- 20 per cent for savings and extra debt repayment
- 30 per cent to spend on wants.

Simplicity is the beauty of this cash-flow strategy. There's no need to analyse how you're currently spending your money or to spend hours each month updating complex spreadsheets. It's also a strategy that you can dive into straight away. Often, getting started is the hardest part – this strategy's set allocation makes implementation easy.

I mentioned before that I'm a visual person; so, here are some diagrams showing the two ways this approach could look for you.

Possible structure 1: two bank accounts

Your savings component (20 per cent) stays in your main bank account (this could be an offset account – I discuss more about these later in the chapter). The money you'll be spending on your needs and wants goes into a 'living' bank account.

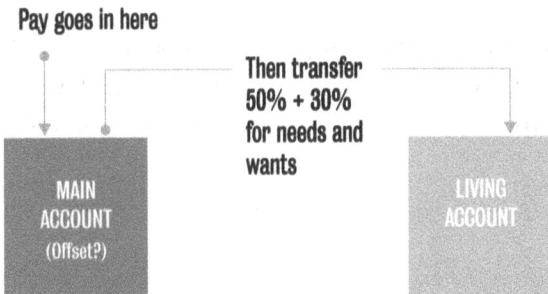

Pay goes in here

Then transfer 50% + 30% for needs and wants

MAIN ACCOUNT (Offset?)

LIVING ACCOUNT

Possible structure 2: three bank accounts

Alternatively, if you're happy to use three bank accounts, the set-up would look like this:

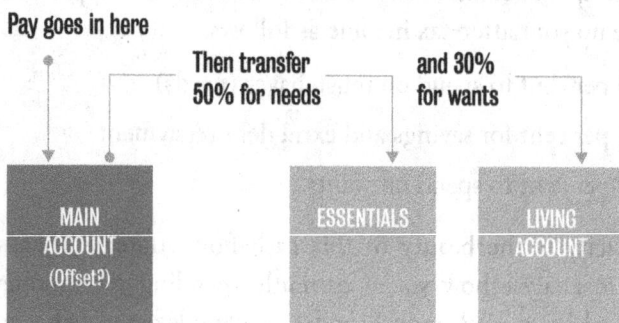

Pay goes in here

Then transfer 50% for needs   and 30% for wants

| MAIN ACCOUNT (Offset?) | ESSENTIALS | LIVING ACCOUNT |

Bills, groceries and home-loan repayments or rent fall into the must-haves category, which in this set-up is paid for from the 'essentials' bank account. Wants are paid for from the 'living' account – things like eating out, going to the movies, buying lunch and lattes, gifts, clothes, holidays and so on.

I encourage you to fine-tune your allocations after running with it a few months. Maybe the right split for you is 30 per cent savings and 20 per cent for wants; or perhaps you have a large mortgage and so need 60 per cent in must-haves. Maybe 60/15/25 is the right answer for you. Don't be afraid to modify it for your circumstances.

One thing to note regarding the 50/20/30 approach, however, is that its rigidity can make it challenging for lower-income-earners, and maybe too easy for higher-income-earners.

THE BUCKET STRATEGY

The bucket strategy has many variations but, as a broad approach, it's probably the most popular of the standard budgeting strategies. As with the 50/20/30 strategy, you have multiple bank accounts, with automatic transfers to each. Unlike 50/20/30, though, the amount of each transfer is determined by you after you have reviewed your current expenses. You make an active decision on where you want your money allocated.

Here's how it looks:

A typical set-up for the bucket strategy

The key elements of the approach are as follows:

- having multiple bank accounts – each with a purpose

- using automated fixed transfers to spread money across the accounts

- needing to first calculate what you're spending on bills and so on in order to determine the amount that should go into each account.

Pay goes in here

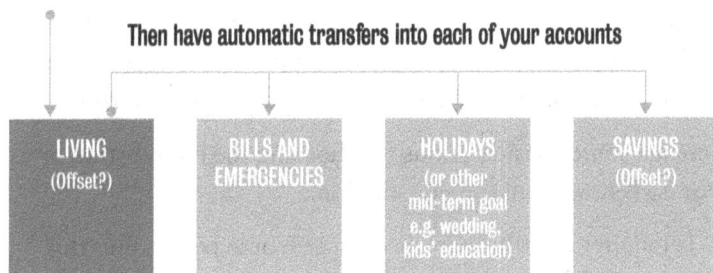

Then have automatic transfers into each of your accounts

| LIVING (Offset?) | BILLS AND EMERGENCIES | HOLIDAYS (or other mid-term goal e.g. wedding, kids' education) | SAVINGS (Offset?) |

A great tool for calculating your spending can be found at the Australian government's MoneySmart website, at www.money smart.gov.au/tools-and-resources/calculators-and-apps/budget-planner.

One element I like about the bucket structure is that when bills come in, you know the cash is sitting there to cover them. You do need to put some seed money into the bills account, though – perhaps a few thousand dollars. Without this, you may hit the same problem as my brother did: a large bill came in not long after he'd set things up, and there wasn't enough in the bills account to cover it.

Also, think about setting an upper limit on how much you want sitting in the savings account – say, $10,000 – an amount that could see you through if you lost your job or something similarly serious befell you. Once you save more than that, you'd want to start investing, something we'll cover in subsequent chapters.

It is possible to implement a bucket strategy virtually – that is, just having a single bank account and tracking your buckets on a spreadsheet or similar. This is especially effective if you have a mortgage and that single account is an offset account, as it means the maximum amount of money possible is sitting against your mortgage, reducing its interest expense and therefore the time until it's repaid. A virtual approach like this does require a bit more work to track things, however, and discipline to not overspend.

Here are some considerations for choosing the bucket strategy as your cash-flow management solution:

- It requires multiple bank accounts – some people find this too complex.

- It requires work up-front to determine appropriate amounts to put in each account.

- Some people find they end up robbing Peter to pay Paul – that is, finding there's not enough in one account and so 'borrowing' from another account to make things work. This can end up a total mess.

- There can be a timing issue with the bills account, as mentioned – an initial float is essential to overcome this.

- It can work well in combination with the reverse budget approach, which we'll look at next.

THE REVERSE BUDGET

The reverse budget is another cash-flow strategy that has the benefit of being easy to implement – an important criterion when the potential for procrastination and inaction is ever-present. Sometimes called 'pay yourself first', the reverse budget dictates that you save a fixed amount, then spend the rest however you like. Pretty easy, right?

The key is to set aside money for savings first. This is the opposite of what most people without a cash-flow plan do. Their plan is to save whatever is left over at the end of the fortnight or month – which, of course, more often than not ends up being zero. Under the reverse budget approach, money goes to savings first, almost like it's another bill. If you're choosing to pay more than the minimum monthly repayment on your home loan, you're implementing this strategy already without even knowing it. Australia's superannuation system is another example, as are the retirement schemes of most other countries.

Here's an example of how a reverse budget might look.

An example set-up for the reverse budget

As this is a strategy that focuses on saving rather than spending, it avoids the need to track where your money goes. Spend your remaining money how you like, but when the amount you've given yourself runs out, you need to survive until next payday.

Pay $3,000 •---------- Auto transfer ----------▶ Savings $800

Live off the rest

As with most cash-flow strategies, automated transfers are an essential ingredient for success. If the savings component is left to personal self-discipline and routine, the potential for failure grows enormously. It's now so easy to automate your financial arrangements, though: why wouldn't you want to take advantage?

If you're comfortable with multiple bank accounts, you could split your savings amount into those. For instance, you might transfer $200 to the mortgage as an extra repayment, $100 to the emergency account, and $100 to the holiday account – bucket strategy–style.

Here are the key considerations when implementing the reverse budget strategy:

- It requires a lot of discipline if you are paid monthly.

- If you're self-employed, you could adjust the strategy to save a percentage of each client payment received instead of a set dollar amount.

- You don't need to work out how much you've been spending in order to get started. Just start with a conservative level of saving and aim to creep it up over time.

- Consider using an offset account for your savings if you have a mortgage.

- There's no need to track spending – a significant appeal of this strategy.

- It offers a good balance between both sides of the cash-flow equation – it doesn't fall into the trap that many other strategies do of putting all the energy into the spending piece.

THE BIG CUT

The big-cut strategy is a no-mucking-around, rip-the-Band-Aid-off approach that I like a lot.

It's really simple: review how you're currently spending your money and find one significant thing that you can eliminate. This isn't easy, though, and typically requires a lifestyle change. It could involve getting rid of one car in the household, or moving to a smaller home so that you become mortgage-free, ceasing all take-away food or giving up a vice like tobacco, alcohol or gambling. Make one big cut, and then live life as normal in all other respects.

This strategy can be particularly useful if you find yourself struggling with your expenses exceeding your income. Your one big cut should deliver you back into a balanced situation; hopefully even into a position where your income exceeds expenses, so that you can save again.

According to the Australian Bureau of Statistics, 2015–16 research into household budgets (via the Household Expenditure Survey) revealed that the big-ticket items for the typical household are as follows:

- housing (including mortgage repayments) – 19.6 per cent

- food and non-alcoholic beverages – 16.6 per cent

- transport – 14.5 per cent

- recreation – 12.1 per cent.

Given we're hunting for one big, significant expenditure cut, it's likely you'll need to take action in one of these four areas.

Here are the things to consider before embarking on the big cut cash-flow strategy:

- It's not painless – it's called the BIG cut for a reason. Cutting out a couple of coffees per week won't do. If there's no pain or lifestyle change, you're not doing it right.

- It's attractive if you have no appetite for doing detailed research into how you're currently spending your money.

- It doesn't require you to track your spending on an ongoing basis.

- It's ideal for someone currently spending more than they're earning. If you're in that situation, you need a lifestyle change.

Before we leave this one, a final thought. It's called 'the big cut', but remember that cash-flow management has two elements, expenses and income. You could flip this strategy and instead of cutting expenses, find a way of making a big leap in your income – by taking a second job or chasing a new, higher-paying role, perhaps. The trick here would be not to fall for the all-too-common problem of lifestyle inflation. For a 'big leap' to propel you along the path to gaining choice, you'd need your expenses to remain unchanged, so that the extra income becomes savings and then wealth.

TRACKING YOUR SPENDING

This is the no-budget budget. I understand that tech-savvy people in particular quite like this strategy, because it works well if you're comfortable using apps to track spending and income.

The name really gives the game away, but to implement the 'track your spending' cash-flow strategy you:

- track where your money goes via an app or spreadsheet
- lock in a time each month to review the data – say, the first Sunday of every month, after dinner. The question to ask yourself is whether you're happy with your choices.

This strategy relies on personal self-reflection and changing your money habits – sometimes, just being conscious of where your money goes is enough to change your habits. Ideally, you want to determine in percentage terms how much of your income is spent on different categories. Most of the money-management apps will do this for you, but if you're uncomfortable providing your bank login details to these providers (I am), you can instead extract your transaction data from your online banking service into a spreadsheet and track things that way.

In addition to checking that you're happy with the spending choices you made in the prior month, you should monitor how your spending changes over time. Hopefully this will show trends that provide positive reinforcement for you.

Note that using the 'track your spending' approach also allows you to easily calculate your net asset position, so you could perhaps review this while you're checking your spending each month.

Some considerations when adopting the 'track your spending' cash-flow strategy:

- It's best for someone who already has a cash-flow surplus (i.e. an income greater than their expenses) and whose focus therefore is on maximising savings. There is no mechanism for limiting spending in this strategy – by the time you conduct your monthly review, the money is already spent.

- The strategy is all about changing habits.

- Ideally, as mentioned, you would track the percentage you spent on different categories – this makes the trends easier to monitor over time.

- This suits a single person better than a couple, as it's tough to debate what's worthwhile spending after it's already been spent. The process could actually be a spark for conflict.

- You need to set aside time to analyse the data each month: it requires discipline.

ZERO-BASED BUDGETING

Zero-based budgeting is the most hardcore of the cash-flow strategies, as it requires work and commitment. However, if you're in a tight spot financially, and especially if your expenses exceed your income and/or you have persistent credit-card debt, this strategy could provide the adrenaline shot you need. It's the approach advocated by Dave Ramsey, a US legend in the personal finance space.

The zero-based budgeting approach requires that you sit down every month and do two things:

1. Review your previous month's spending against your plan for that month – how did you go and what can you learn?

2. Create a new spending plan for how to spend every dollar in the upcoming month.

Here's an example of how it might look:

A zero-based budget example

You can see that every dollar coming in has been allocated to expenses or savings in advance. For large annual expenses like Christmas presents, you can put a little away each month for several months, or perhaps all year.

Spending plan

Month: June	$
Income	4,750
Expenses:	
Mortage	1,650
Gas	440
Electricity	–
Rates	–
Water	225
Internet	95
Groceries	1,570
Other food	200
Music lessons	120
Hair	–
Clothing	–
Entertainment	300
Savings	150
TOTAL	4,750

Expenses (including savings) exactly match income – zero left over

The great thing about zero-based budgeting is that you gain a great sense of where your money is going, and so you can be very deliberate in how you spend your money.

Here's what to consider if you plan on adopting the zero-based budgeting strategy:

- It's a great strategy if you currently spend more than you earn – it's a shock treatment.

- Some people report finding it unsustainable, however – too much work to continue with. It might still be valuable to do for three to six months if it helps you get your spending better aligned to your income.

- It could make you into the fun police. Will you have to be the household grouch to make this one work?

* * *

Still not sure which strategy is right for you? Complete the self-assessment on page 7 or in the workbook for my suggestion of the strategy most likely to be successful for you.

WHY MOST BUDGETS FAIL

Most budgets fail for the same reason most diets fail: they're not sustainable long term. The three typical reasons are:

1. The budget is too much work to maintain.

2. Unexpected bills blow your plans up.

3. It feels like living in a straitjacket.

Essentially, what happens is that the chosen budget strategy doesn't suit the individual trying to use it. That's why I've explained not one, but six different approaches – something to suit everyone.

Here are three tips to address these common failure points and help ensure your budget plan successfully progresses you along the journey to gaining choice:

1. When choosing an approach, be realistic about the time and discipline you have to maintain it. Some of the strategies require you to sit down for an hour or two each month; others require up-front work to ascertain where your money is currently being spent. Some others, however, you could have up and running in minutes. Pick the approach you're most likely to be able to stick with.

2. Plan for unexpected expenses. Sometimes people get very energised and set up a great budget, but then a week later the car goes in for a service, a problem is found, and a $1,200 bill hits the table. That wasn't in the budget! Hands are thrown up in the air and the whole exercise is discarded with, 'I knew budgeting wouldn't work for me'. Be aware of this pitfall and plan for it. Ideally, you'll have some savings already, and you can access these in the case of a large unexpected expense. Alternatively, perhaps a credit card is the short-term answer – just have a plan for how it will be cleared.

3. Be clear about your goals and realistic about your savings rate to address the straitjacket problem. Budgeting can seem like dieting: there can be a sense that a budget, just like a diet, sucks the joy out of life. However, as discussed in chapter 1, making progress towards your goals will bring happiness. Let's say one of your goals is a trip to the Maldives to snorkel the reefs. Sure, it might necessitate cutting back on buying lunches at work, but the happiness you'll experience on that trip, and the memories you'll have forever, will produce bucketloads more happiness than what you've foregone.

A realistic savings rate will ensure that you can still spend money on the things that make you happy. The aim isn't to cut out all spending and live like a monk! You're just trying to cut down on the expenses that have crept into your life but provide little joy – most often linked to keeping up with what others around you are spending money on.

There's no need for you to become the next person to kick off a budget strategy with great intentions, and then two weeks later be complaining to your friends about how it didn't work. Use the self-assessment tool to point you in the right direction, and choose a strategy that you can sustain long term. Then, have a little patience. Change always feels uncomfortable to begin with, but stick with it and you'll be wishing you'd gotten your cash flow sorted out years ago!

Apps and tools to help you succeed

We (typically) walk around with a powerful computer in our pocket – our phone – and banking is easy to do online. Combined, these two developments have created a fertile environment for the development of clever tools that help us make the most of our money.

The Mint app has long been popular in the US, but sadly it hasn't been rolled out beyond North America. Here in Australia, two apps with confusingly similar names provide much the same functionality – Pocketbook and PocketSmith. These apps link with your bank accounts and help you easily categorise what you've spent your money on. Armed with this information, strategies like 'track your spending' and zero-based budgeting become a whole lot easier.

Increasingly, the banks' free apps also provide this functionality, so if you have all (or at least most) of your financial accounts with the one institution, perhaps check their app out as a starting point.

Rounding-up apps are a useful way for people to save. As you spend money, this kind of app rounds up your purchase to the nearest dollar, and then makes it easy to invest these accumulated round-ups. Acorns was the pioneer and remains a big player in the US; newer arrivals include Chime and Qapital. In Australia, Acorns became Raiz, though it continues to deliver the same service. Again, banks are also beginning to offer this rounding-up-savings functionality, with ING, the Commonwealth Bank, and new player Up all offering these solutions to their customers.

If you think any of these apps might suit you, why not give them a trial?

PART THREE
INVEST IN STOCKS

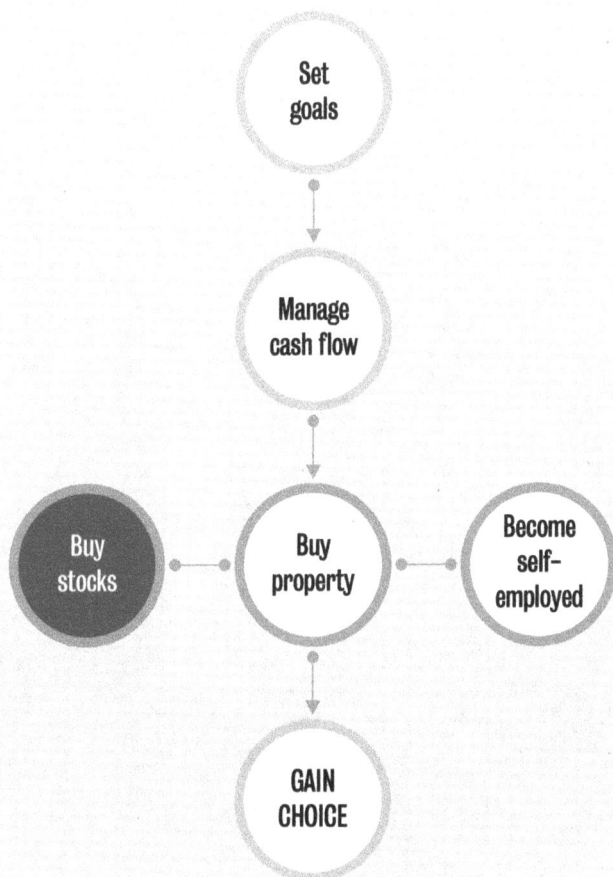

```
                    ┌──────────┐
                    │   Set    │
                    │  goals   │
                    └────┬─────┘
                         │
                         ▼
                    ┌──────────┐
                    │  Manage  │
                    │ cash flow│
                    └────┬─────┘
                         │
                         ▼
   ┌────────┐       ┌──────────┐       ┌──────────┐
   │  Buy   │──────▶│   Buy    │◀─────▶│  Become  │
   │ stocks │       │ property │       │  self-   │
   └────────┘       └────┬─────┘       │ employed │
                         │             └──────────┘
                         ▼
                    ┌──────────┐
                    │  GAIN    │
                    │  CHOICE  │
                    └──────────┘
```

4

STOCK MARKET FOUNDATIONS

Many of the richest people in the world have built their wealth through stocks, with Warren Buffett, the octogenarian from Omaha, being perhaps the best known. Stocks (or 'shares', if you prefer – the terms are interchangeable) provide the most accessible way for individuals to build wealth. There are apps available now that allow you to start investing with as little as $50! Using exchange traded funds (ETFs, which we'll discuss later in this chapter), that $50 could be spread across hundreds or even thousands of different companies.

Stocks have many benefits:

- They're liquid and divisible. 'Liquid' in the sense that they can be sold for cash quickly, usually in three days. They're 'divisible' in that when you sell, you don't need to sell your entire holding, only as many stocks as you need to raise the cash required.

- They're near effortless to own. Once you've bought them, you can forget about them. The company's management and staff do the actual work – you just sit back and collect your dividends.

- They don't wear out. In fact, your stock investments have an in-built growth mechanism. Companies almost never pay out their entire profit as dividends. Instead, they retain some of the profit to reinvest into the business to help it grow – updating premises, buying out a competitor, conducting R&D or undertaking a new marketing program.

Of the three pathways to financial autonomy, I've started with stocks for all of these reasons. Many people begin their financial autonomy journey investing in stocks, and stocks may remain their primary tool to gain choice. Alternatively, maybe down the road a little, their stock portfolio provides the capital to enable them to start a business or buy property.

Whatever investment strategy you develop, a working knowledge of stock market investing is a must. So let's get you up to speed.

WHAT IS A STOCK?

A stock is part-ownership – a share – in a business. When you become a stockholder, you acquire the rights of a part-owner of that business. You can vote on the directors running the business. You may receive a share of the profits of the business via dividends. If the company needs to raise new capital to fund growth, you get the first opportunity to buy the new shares issued. You also benefit, as the company grows, from a (hopefully) rising stock price.

Significantly, you enjoy the benefits of ownership, but you take on almost none of the risk. If the company gets sued, or defaults on a loan, you're not liable. In the worst case, the company could go broke and you'd lose the value of your stocks in that company, but this occurrence is fortunately very rare.

HOW DO STOCKS MAKE YOU MONEY?

Stocks make you money in two ways:

1. dividends

2. price growth.

Companies make profits – most of the time, anyway! A portion of the profit may be paid out to stockholders as dividends, and the company retains the remainder to reinvest into the business and generate growth. A business such as a pharmaceuticals company that needs to constantly invest in research to find new drugs might pay out 50 per cent of its profits as dividends and retain 50 per cent to fund growth. A mature business, by contrast, perhaps a bank, might pay out 90 per cent of its profits as dividends and only reinvest 10 per cent.

This reinvestment process typically leads to business growth, and as the business grows, its stock price rises. When you sell your stocks, you receive the benefit of that price appreciation. (Until you sell, these are 'paper profits', meaning theoretical profits on paper only.) This is called 'price growth', 'capital growth' or just 'growth'.

It's important, then, to always be cognisant of your total return as a stockholder:

Total return = dividends + growth

Depending on your strategy goals, a company paying a low dividend may be a perfectly good investment if the growth is sufficiently attractive. In fact often, from a tax perspective, growth is preferable to income, as you don't pay tax until you sell the stock and receive the proceeds, and capital gains are often taxed at a lower rate than income.

Financial autonomy in action: How I got started

Often, getting started is the hardest part, so I thought I might share with you how I got started in investing. Each of our journeys is unique, of course, but the thing I hope you take away is that you don't need thousands and thousands of dollars or a PhD in finance to make a start.

I first owned stocks when I was a teenager in high school: my grandfather gifted some of the CSR stocks that he'd received as an employee to his nine grandchildren. It wasn't a huge amount of money, from memory, about $500 worth I think, but I was rapt.

CSR, an Australian conglomerate with interests at the time across building products, sugar refining and mining, had a program where you could buy more stocks each month – a fixed amount like $100 or $200. I was working as a casual at Coles Supermarkets at the time and had a little cash available, so I signed up. My first regular savings plan.

Later, when it was time to do my high-school work experience placement, I wrote to stockbroking firms and secured two weeks' work at a brokerage in Melbourne's Collins Street. This was back in the days when the stock exchange consisted of hundreds of people (almost exclusively men), yelling at each other. One of my jobs was to take the orders over the phone from the stockbroker's office, and then run and find our dealer so he could buy or sell. What a rush!

After high school, I started work at the (then government-run) Commonwealth Bank; not long after I started, the federal government decided to sell the business off in a public float. I participated. They even had an interest-free loan for staff to help them buy the stocks, with repayments coming directly out of their pay (my first experience of gearing, though I had no idea that's what I was doing at the time).

I moved out of home at 21. My income was pretty low, but I kept my expenses down living in share houses, and continued to buy stocks when I could. At age 24, I was able to buy my first home. It was an ugly, brown-brick flat, but it was a start, an essential foundation stone upon which my financial position today was built. (Check out episode 25 of the Financial Autonomy podcast for how that particular transaction unfolded.) The purchase was possible because I'd accumulated stocks over about a decade with small chunks of money here and there. I sold those stocks to get the deposit.

Investing in stocks set me on the path to financial autonomy – and the opportunity is still there for those prepared to invest today. In fact, the online tools available now make investing in stocks more accessible than ever.

ARE STOCKS RISKY?

If you've never invested in stocks before, there's a very good chance you have a perception that stock market investment is risky – perhaps just a small step up from betting on the horse races. The reality is that a diversified portfolio of stocks, held for an appropriate amount of time (ideally five years plus) is one of the lowest risk investments you can make. Here's why:

- Looking at rolling five-year periods from 1990 until July 2019, there was only one instance of a negative return on the

Australian stock market. That occurred if you were unlucky enough to invest all of your money just before the global financial crisis (GFC) in 2008: your return over five years would have been –3.04 per cent. Every other five-year period produced positive returns, with the average result being 10.14 per cent.

In the US over the same period, the average return was much the same: 10.8 per cent. In addition to the post-GFC period, the US also had negative five-year returns in the early 2000s, after the tech wreck, though the damage then was approximately –2.4 per cent.

- Dividends across a diversified portfolio are very stable, so even if prices move around, your income remains steady.

- It's easy to diversify. We'll explore this more shortly, but one of the attractions of stock investment is that you can have exposure to retail businesses, manufacturers, IT innovators, service providers, and plenty more. Even when tough times befall one company or industry sector, another sector will be on the rise.

- Liquidity. If something changes in your life, stocks can be sold and you've got your money in three days.

- They keep pace with inflation – something bank deposits don't achieve.

Stock market volatility, rather than being a negative, can provide an opportunity. At the time of writing, we saw markets fall as COVID-19 spread around the world. Those who continued to invest through this period picked up stocks at prices that will almost certainly look attractive five to ten years from now.

So how has the myth arisen that stocks are risky? Mainly, it's come from the daily stock market reporting in the media.

Driving to work, you might hear that the S&P 500 (the US stock market index) dropped 100 points overnight – and you conclude the world is coming to an end. The fact that this is a move of less than a third of one per cent doesn't register; nor does the media mention that the S&P 500 had gained 800 points in the previous three months. Daily stock market price movements are just noise, useful to no-one. They merely fill space in media programs.

Stock price volatility is risky, it's true, if you're forced to sell at a time when markets are down. This type of risk though – volatility – should actually be viewed as your friend. The reason you earn 8 to 10 per cent on your stock investments but close to zero on your cash in the bank is because you're being compensated as a stock investor for putting up with the volatility associated with stocks. Brian Portnoy, in his book *The Geometry of Wealth*, writes: 'Volatility is the emotional cost of achieving the growth we seek'.

Behaviour problems

The academic discipline of behavioural finance has developed over the past couple of decades, and provides some interesting insights into common human actions that are detrimental to investment success:

- We feel loss more acutely than an equivalent gain: our in-built reaction to a loss of 20 per cent, for example, is far stronger than our reaction to a 20 per cent gain. Research suggests we 'feel' the loss around twice as much as the gain. Armed with this knowledge, take an extra few moments to reflect on whether the risk of a given investment strategy is truly tolerable. The consequence of this bias, known as 'loss aversion', is that in times of uncertainty, investors are inclined to sell, despite having no need to do so. They lock in losses and inevitably miss the recovery.

- We also tend to want to stick with the crowd – known as 'herding bias' – even if the crowd is heading in a direction that isn't where we want to go.

- We seek out only opinions that agree with our own – 'confirmation bias' – which is an issue far broader than just investing.

- We also tend to disproportionately be influenced by recent events – 'recency bias'. Because the stock market fell 2 per cent last month, we reason it's more likely to go down this month, or vice versa.

An awareness of these ingrained human vulnerabilities may enable you to recognise and resist them.

The other mechanism through which the myth of stock market risk spreads is the story of someone's uncle's cousin's next-door neighbour who lost everything on the stock market. In my 20-plus years of talking to people about investing, I've never met anyone who has actually suffered this fate. I have, however, met some people who have 'lost' money on the stock market. Here's how it looks:

- They put $100,000 into the stock market.

- It rose to $130,000. They were happy.

- It fell to $120,000. They were less happy.

- They concluded the world was about to end and sold.

- The stock market is terrible because they 'lost' $10,000.

Now, of course, it could happen that the fall comes first rather than a rise, but my experience is that people are more willing to stick with things in this case – they want to wait until they're at least back to where they started before they think of selling.

Here are some other ways people lose money in stocks:

- They buy high-risk, speculative companies, usually businesses that aren't making a profit.

- They don't diversify, so one poor outcome has a large impact.

- They borrow to invest and make one of the two mistakes above or just haven't done their numbers on what is affordable.

No-one, and certainly not you, should ever lose money investing in stocks. All the mistakes mentioned arise through human frailty and ignorance; the stock market itself is not the culprit. I can't recall who said it, but there's a great quote which is spot on: 'The stock market is a mechanism for redistributing wealth from the impatient to the patient'.

Interesting stock market facts

- The first stock market was in Amsterdam in 1602.

- Approximately 630,000 companies are traded publicly throughout the world.

- The NYSE conducts 1.6 billion trades on average every day (at time of writing). It conducted its first trade in 1792.

- Of the 200 companies included in the S&P/ASX 200, the top 10 make up 41 per cent at time of writing.

- In Somalia, pirates established a stock exchange to allow locals to finance their hijacking raids.

- The terms 'bull market' and 'bear market', which are commonly used to describe upward- and downward-trending periods in stock market cycles, derive from fights organised by Spanish soldiers between Spanish bulls and Californian grizzly bears. They noticed that bulls thrust up to attack, while bears struck downwards.

DIVERSIFICATION

Perhaps the greatest benefit of building wealth through stock market investing is the ease with which you can diversify. 'Diversifying' means spreading your investments so as to reduce risk. Here's an example:

- Option 1 – you invest $10,000 into stock A.

- Option 2 – you split your $10,000 across stocks A, B and C, with a third of the money going to each. This is the diversified option.

If all stocks rose or fell by the same percentage, then it would make no difference which of these two options you chose. However, it's extremely unlikely that three different stocks will have identical outcomes. Here are three different scenarios so you can get a sense of the impact of diversification.

First scenario

Growth outcomes: stock A rises 6 per cent, stock B falls 5 per cent, stock C rises 11 per cent:

- Option 1 (no diversification) delivers 6 per cent.
- Option 2 (with diversification) delivers 7.3 per cent.

The diversified portfolio can withstand one poor performer and still deliver a good result.

Second scenario

Growth outcomes: stock A falls 12 per cent, B falls 3 per cent, C falls 14 per cent:

- Option 1 delivers –12 per cent.
- Option 2 delivers –9.6 per cent.

In a broadly falling market, the diversified portfolio may mitigate the impact somewhat.

Third scenario

Growth outcomes: stock A rises 20 per cent, B rises 3 per cent, C falls 2 per cent:

- Option 1 delivers 20 per cent.
- Option 2 delivers 6.9 per cent.

If you bet on one stock and it has extraordinary returns, no diversification delivers the superior outcome. This is perhaps a bit like betting on black in roulette – great when it works, but hardly the basis of a long-term strategy.

If you construct a portfolio of individual stocks, you would typically have 10 to 20 different companies within the portfolio, ensuring that poor performance from one or two companies would not be catastrophic. Alternatively, you might choose to invest in the stock market through a fund, perhaps via your retirement savings, or with an exchange traded fund (ETF), which we will discuss shortly. These funds will have hundreds and sometimes thousands of individual companies within their portfolios, eliminating the potential for one or two bad apples to spoil the bunch.

Diversification can take several forms when investing in stocks. Not only can you diversify across individual businesses, you can also spread your investments across different industry sectors – finance, resources, health care, telecommunications and consumer staples, for instance. Each industry sector performs differently across the economic cycle. When the economy is booming, for instance, the finance sector might perform strongly due to higher demand for loans, but in a recession, it might be health care or consumer staples that hold up best.

You can also diversify across large, well-established businesses and smaller up-and-comers, and businesses that are entirely focused on their local market versus those that operate around the globe. In fact, via ETFs you can gain exposure to stocks in every corner of the world. An investor living in Singapore can quite easily invest in US, Indian, or Japanese stocks via ETFs.

Stock investors can diversify into property investment via the many different listed property trusts – businesses that are professional landlords, typically of commercial properties such as office towers or shopping malls. In recent years, ETFs have even been created that enable stock market investors to buy bonds (fixed-interest loans to governments or large corporates) and commodities like gold. The ability to build an investment portfolio to fit your view of the world and your appetite for risk is really quite incredible.

WHAT DO STOCK MARKETS DO?

Stock markets enable investors to exchange their stocks with one another. They're platforms that bring together buyers and sellers. Most markets are in fact formally called 'exchanges' – the New York Stock Exchange for instance – and this word 'exchange' encapsulates their function.

The operator of a given stock exchange will set rules that all participants must follow. For example, exchange operators will require companies they list on their market to release information in a timely manner and in a way that ensures all investors and potential investors have access. This is to prevent insiders having an unfair advantage, which dissuades other investors from participating in the market. The market operators will also stipulate how settlement is to occur between buyers and sellers, and broadly endeavour to ensure activities are fair to all participants. This engenders trust in the market, which benefits everyone through strong investor participation.

WHAT DO BROKERS DO?

A common question from new investors is, 'Do I need to set up a brokerage account to invest in stocks?' To buy individual stocks or ETFs, the answer is yes. You can gain access to stock markets via managed funds (called 'mutual funds' in the United States) or via your retirement savings without opening a brokerage account, but for the purposes of getting to your financial autonomy goal, you'll need a stock trading account – a brokerage account.

Once upon a time, establishing a brokerage account required scheduling a meeting with someone in a suit, typically in an office with either lots of wood and sombre tones, or plenty of glass and views of the city skyline. You would then appeal to them to invest your money.

Fortunately, a lot has changed in the past 20 to 30 years. Brokerage accounts are now opened online in minutes. They cost nothing to establish and the cost per transaction is a tiny fraction of what it was in the old days. Many of the online brokerage accounts include access to research and market data, which is genuinely valuable. They also provide a way for you to monitor your portfolio. When you want to buy or sell, you simply enter your instructions into their platform, and the broker takes care of the rest, settling the transaction via your bank account a few days later.

Brokers are registered with the stock exchanges and must comply with their rules and requirements. Investors cannot buy stocks directly on the stock exchange – they must go through a broker. This ensures that everyone trading can have confidence that the other party can deliver on their side of the transaction. The broker is effectively vouching for their clients that they either have the cash to make the purchase or have the stocks that they're offering for sale. If the client can't deliver, the brokers must make it good.

EXCHANGE TRADED FUNDS

Two things have been enormous in the stock market investing space over the past two decades. The first is online stock broking, as just mentioned, which massively increased access for investors and slashed costs. The second has been exchange traded funds, referred to everywhere as 'ETFs'.

Managed or mutual funds have been around for a very long time. The first modern-day mutual fund, the Massachusetts Investors Trust, was launched in 1924. These funds enable investors to pool their savings and invest across a broader spread of stocks than they could have purchased cost-effectively themselves. However, they rely heavily on the person or team running the fund to choose the stocks in the portfolio wisely. Successful fund managers tend to be very well rewarded; those that underperform go out of business quietly.

In the past, getting into and out of these funds required paper-based applications and could take weeks. They often had considerable costs embedded into them, too, meaning that even if the portfolio produced a 10 per cent return, the investors might only get 7 to 8 per cent after management fees and other costs.

Then, in 1974, a guy named Jack Bogle came along and launched something called an 'index fund'. It had the same entry and exit paperwork as all the other funds going around, but instead of employing fund managers to choose which stocks to buy and sell, his fund simply replicated an index. They looked at the S&P 500 index – the index of the 500 largest companies in the United States, weighted according to the size of each company – and simply copied it. This meant there was no need to employ expensive fund managers, and no chance of underperforming the market (although no chance of outperforming either). Bogle pushed through enormous initial scepticism, largely from vested interests in the investment community, to see his company – Vanguard – become one the largest fund managers in the world by the time of his death in 2019.

The holdings within traditional managed funds were a closely kept secret, as each fund endeavoured to beat the other. In the index fund space, by contrast, the holdings within the portfolio were known to all.

Exchange traded funds are simply index funds that can be bought and sold on a stock exchange, through a stockbroker, instead of having to deal with the paperwork of going through the fund manager directly. Before index funds, however, attempts to get funds listed on exchanges had limited success, because the value (or price) that those funds then traded for did not necessarily reflect the actual value of their portfolios. This was the result of portfolio holdings being secret – investors just had to guess at the underlying value, and recognise that future performance was a bet on the fund manager in charge.

The transparency of index funds overcame this. ETFs have market makers sitting behind them, constantly ensuring the price listed to buy or sell an ETF accurately reflects the true value of all the stocks the fund owns.

Index-style funds already had lower costs than traditional funds, as mentioned, because they didn't need expensive analysts and fund managers – but as they got bigger and bigger, costs tumbled. Today, investors can use ETFs to access markets right around the world. The management costs are negligible, and you can be in or out in seconds.

Newer ETFs don't only follow standard indexes. Some use different filters to select their stocks, and some even have active fund managers like the traditional funds which preceded them. ETFs that only hold companies deemed 'sustainable' have gained considerable popularity, as have those focused on particular sectors like health care or IT.

When developing your investment strategy, give plenty of thought to whether ETFs might be a good vehicle through which to gain your stock market exposure. Sure, they won't skyrocket in value like that little mining company you take a punt on that happens to find gold, but they also won't collapse into oblivion. With an ETF, you get what's on the label. It will be broadly diversified, and at a cost that is barely noticeable.

5

INVESTMENT SELECTION AND STRATEGY

When investing, you want the simplest, most-likely-to-succeed option there is. And that means focusing on what really matters.

Brian Portnoy (who I interviewed in episode 64 of the podcast) makes a great analogy in his book *The Geometry of Wealth*. He's at an airport and there's a food court. He's hungry, but there are so many options – lots of different restaurants, and each with many different items to choose from: burgers, sushi, Chinese and pizza. He could look through the menus of each establishment until he finds the dish that makes his mouth water – but instead, he narrows his choices. He likes Mexican food, so he heads to the Mexican restaurant and, after a quick scan of their menu, orders a nice pulled-pork burrito with extra salsa.

The most important decision for him to make is the type of cuisine he wants. Once he's made that decision, there's not that much difference between a pulled-pork burrito and a beef burrito.

If he gets the choice of restaurant right, his chances of eating a meal that makes him happy are pretty high.

In the investment universe, the equivalent of getting the restaurant right is your 'asset allocation'. Do you want to have 50 per cent of your investment in growth assets, such as stocks and property, and 50 per cent in defensive assets like cash and bonds? Or would a 90/10 split be more to your taste? If you have clarity on your asset allocation, you can then consider which specific investments to choose.

Your asset-allocation decision is influenced by your goal, the time frame that you have, and your personal comfort level with volatility. Here's a rough guide to the link between asset allocation and time frame:

Investment time frame (years)	Growth asset allocation	Defensive asset allocation
1	0%	100%
2	25%	75%
3	50%	50%
5+	100%	0%

Time frame isn't the only consideration in your asset-allocation decision. Plenty of people have an investment time frame of greater than five years, yet choose to have an asset allocation of less than 100 per cent growth assets – perhaps something like 80/20 – because they like the smoothing effect of having some defensive assets in the mix (as illustrated in the section on diversification in chapter 4).

In this chapter, we are exploring stocks as your pathway to financial autonomy, but it's worth mentioning again that via funds like ETFs you can actually access a wide range of different asset classes. You have the ability to completely customise a strategy to suit your risk tolerance and needs. Let's say you wanted a portfolio that was 50 per cent growth and 50 per cent defensive assets. You could use ETFs to buy bond funds, both domestic and global, to meet your low-risk, defensive quota, and then buy other ETFs to gain exposure to property and stocks around the globe for your growth allocation.

WHAT TO BUY?

Say that you've determined the asset allocation that makes sense for your goal and time frame. How will you fill those asset-allocation buckets? Let's first look at the main options you have:

Growth assets	Defensive assets
Domestic stocks	Cash
Global stocks	Government bonds
Property	Corporate bonds
Infrastructure	Hybrids
Private equity	
Commodities	

All these assets are available via fund structures such as ETFs. Some assets – stocks, property and certainly cash, can be purchased directly. Global stocks are most practically purchased via funds. It's becoming easier to buy stocks on overseas markets but, with so many to choose from, making an informed decision is extremely challenging. Domestic stocks, however, are accessible directly. Those with sufficient interest can build their own portfolio of individual stocks, gaining total control over buying and selling decisions, with the implications for costs and tax.

For those with the inclination, the ability to deep dive into individual stocks in this internet era is bottomless. However, I suggest you at least start your filtering with two key metrics:

1. dividend yield

2. PE ratio.

The dividend yield is the income provided by dividends paid by the company, expressed as a percentage. If you had $10,000 in a given stock and it had a dividend yield of 5 per cent, you would expect to receive $500 per year in dividend income.

Now, of course, company dividends change over time depending upon the profitability of the business. You will therefore often see research reports showing the dividend yield based on the most recently paid dividends, and then including a second figure based on forecast dividends for the year ahead.

The dividend yield is insightful when comparing one stock to another, but it's also useful in comparing one investment to another. For instance, you could weigh up buying a stock that pays a 4 per cent dividend yield versus keeping your money in the bank, where interest of perhaps 1 per cent is paid. If you feel that the extra return gained through dividends is enough to compensate you for the volatility risk associated with stocks, then any growth achieved by the stock is a bonus.

You could make a similar comparison between the dividend yield of a stock and the rental yield produced by an investment property. These markets tend to move in different rhythms. Astute investors can at times spot opportunities where one is mispriced relative to the other using simple numbers like yield.

Price earnings ratios (PE) are more stock-specific. The ratio is determined by dividing the price per share by the earnings per share (EPS) of that company. Here's an example:

Company ABC has a current stock price of $30.

Its earnings per share are $1.50.

This company's PE ratio is 30 ÷ 1.5 = 20.

PEs are particularly helpful when comparing one company to another. A company's stock price tells you nothing about the merits of the business – one company might trade at $5, another at $500. That tells you nothing useful about the companies, it's simply a function of how many stocks are on issue. The PE ratio, though, enables you to compare the two businesses. Let's look at an example:

	Share price	PE ratio
Company A	$5	18.7
Company B	$500	21.1

With the PE data, we can see that Company B is currently more highly valued by the market, with a price over 21 times its current yearly earnings. Company A isn't far behind, though, despite the significant disparity in price, changing hands for almost 19 times its annual earnings. PE ratios tell you a lot about the market's current view of a company. A high PE indicates the market expects earnings to rise, whereas a lower PE implies a less favourable view of the business's future.

Using PE ratios to compare companies within the same sector can also be very useful. Here, we're comparing four banks:

	PE ratio
Bank A	12.3
Bank B	14.1
Bank C	13.2
Bank D	16.8

The PE ratios are telling us that the market currently views Bank D as having the best future prospects – that's the bank for which they're prepared to pay the highest multiple of earnings. Bank A is the least favoured, with the market currently paying a considerably lower multiple. If you were constructing a stock portfolio and wanted to include at least one bank, you'd want to consider these numbers and form a view as to whether they were right. You might, for instance, come to the belief that Bank C, not D, actually had the best growth prospects, and given this outlook, the PE suggests it's undervalued relative to its peers.

PUTTING THE TWO TOGETHER

Looking at the dividend yields and PE ratios together can provide considerable insight into the market's assessment of a business, and help you in building your portfolio. In the table opposite, I've listed ten stocks that you could potentially invest in.

There's an enormous amount that we can draw from just these two pieces of data on each company. From the PE ratios, we can see that the market rates Company D the most highly – people are prepared to pay almost 28 times current earnings and accept a dividend of only 1.9 per cent to buy this stock. That tells you the market feels this company is poised for considerable growth. Sure, they're paying over 27 times earnings now, but if earnings double over the next few years, it's worth it.

	PE ratio	Dividend yield
Company A	12.7	4.2%
Company B	15.6	3.1%
Company C	14.0	4.3%
Company D	27.6	1.9%
Company E	15.2	3.6%
Company F	19.8	2.9%
Company G	11.9	8.8%
Company H	16.1	3.9%
Company I	14.4	4.0%
Company J	15.1	3.8%

Conversely, the most unloved stock in this cohort is Company G: investors are only prepared to pay 11.9 times its earnings. The dividend yield on this stock looks very attractive, though, at 8.8 per cent. These numbers suggest the market expects earnings to drop and dividends to be cut.

As a stock-picking investor, your job is to decide whether you think the market is right. The stock market is a voting contest. Markets regularly go too far, either positively or negatively, and there are successful investors who make their living identifying companies like G, for which market pessimism is overdone. There are others who look for the D-type companies, where strong growth in the future generates strong returns. Alternatively, you might pick out one of the other companies if you feel the market hasn't currently recognised its growth potential.

Here are some reference points on the US and Australian stock markets over the past 30 years to help you assess companies' PE ratios and dividend yields:

- The median PE ratio for the S&P 500 = 14.76.
- The median dividend yield for the S&P 500 = 4.28 per cent.
- The median PE ratio for the S&P/ASX 200 = 15.1.
- The median dividend yield for the S&P/ASX 200 = 4.2 per cent.

Your goals also have a role to play in how you use these numbers to construct your portfolio. Are you looking for growth, or is income your priority? With a growth focus, it may be that companies with higher PE ratios are appealing, whereas if you're an income investor, you might place greater weight on the dividend yield.

There are plenty of other metrics you can look at, of course – 'price-to-book ratio' and 'earnings growth' are popular. However, a working understanding of dividend yield and PE ratios will arm you with enough knowledge to at least perform some initial filtering and narrow down your potential stock investments from thousands to a handful.

CORE-SATELLITE INVESTING

The 'core-satellite' approach to portfolio construction is a popular strategy that we apply with many of our clients. The idea is to have the bulk of your portfolio in more stable, low-risk holdings, and then have some smaller, higher risk (and potentially higher reward) investments to complement these core holdings. Like this:

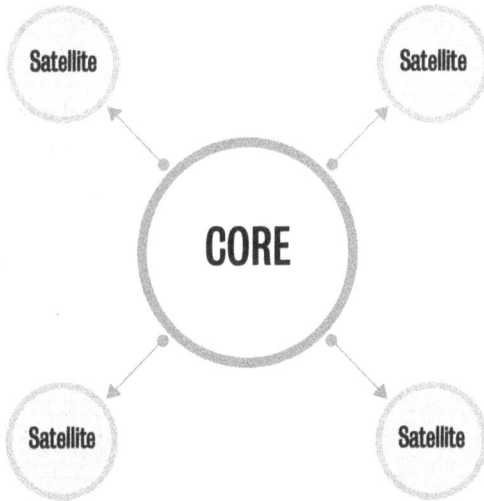

You might, for instance, have funds such as ETFs as your core, so that you have well diversified, broad market exposure. You then look to complement this with some individual stock selections that make up your satellites. The goal with these holdings is to potentially identify a stock set for huge growth that you can ride and get above-average returns from. By holding these as satellites, however, even if they fizzle into nothingness, they aren't significant enough in your portfolio to do lasting damage.

Instead of individual stocks, of course, your satellites could be industry- or country-specific funds. So, you might have some broad funds in your core, and then an ETF for the Taiwanese market or the global biotech industry as your satellites, for example.

Doubling maths

A really helpful mental shortcut when developing your investment strategy is to think about how long it will take for your investment to double. Take a look at the numbers below:

Earnings rate	Years it will take for your money to double
1%	69.7
2%	35
3%	23.4
4%	17.7
5%	14.2
6%	11.9
7%	10.2
8%	9
9%	8
10%	7.3
11%	6.6
12%	6.1

These numbers highlight the danger of being too conservative. If you leave your money in the bank, growth will be excruciatingly slow. If you were a 'balanced' investor – that is, with 50 per cent growth assets and 50 per cent defensive assets – and you moved to 100 per cent growth assets, you could wipe more than four years off the time it will take for your money to double.

To put this another way, if you had 21 years until retirement and $300,000 in retirement savings, by choosing a balanced option, your savings would likely grow to around $1.2 million. That is, they would have doubled twice – from $300,000 to $600,000, and then again from $600,000 to $1.2 million. (I'm ignoring new contributions here.)

If, instead, you chose a more aggressive option that produced a 10 per cent return, your funds would have had the chance to double three times. Now your $300,000 starting balance would become $2.4 million over the same time frame. Notice the disproportionate impact of one extra doubling: that's compounding at work, a concept that's sometimes difficult to grasp.

These numbers also highlight the benefit of having a long time frame. In large part, Warren Buffett's enormous wealth is attributable to the fact that he started investing in his teens and has continued for more than 70 years – that's lots of potential doubling. Time is your friend when it comes to investing, and procrastination is costly.

So, does that mean we should all gravitate to the most aggressive investment options? No. More aggressive investments are more volatile, and depending on your timing, may present a higher risk of suffering a loss. However, it does mean that you need to consider your investment time frame carefully, and if you have a long time frame, seriously question whether defensive assets provide any utility at all.

INVESTING VS TRADING

You're investing in stocks to achieve a specific outcome – achieving financial autonomy and gaining choice in life. You're not buying stocks for entertainment, or as a substitute for a lottery ticket. Predictability of outcome, then, is an important foundational element of your strategy. But how can stock investments deliver predictability? They're up and down every day, right?

Being a long-term investor rather than a short-term speculator is the solution to this riddle. While stocks are volatile day to day, performance over ten-year periods is pretty predictable – you're likely to get 8 to 10 per cent, assuming you're appropriately diversified. There are no guarantees, of course – the timing of your starting point has an impact if you have a single lump sum to work with. Broadly, though, if you buy a diversified portfolio and forget about it for ten years, you can be pretty confident that when you think to look at it again it will have more than doubled.

What you want to avoid is short-term trading – buying and selling within days, weeks, or even months. This is a losing strategy for you for three reasons:

1. **Cost**
   Even though brokerage is cheap these days, it's not zero. Also, there's a difference between the buy and sell price, which acts as an additional trading cost.

2. **Tax**
   Anything you sell at a profit will have a tax liability flow from it. This means you have less money to play with for your next investments.

3. **Competition**
   Some people make their living short-term trading. They run computers that can do thousands of trades per second, 24 hours a day. Do you really think you can beat them? Good luck.

Investors buy stakes in companies that make sense to them, and then hold them to gain their share of the profits through dividends and growth in price. This is the space you want to be in.

Don't be your own enemy

You could easily overlook human behaviour when you're thinking about the keys to successful investing. That would be a huge mistake.

For the 20 years ending in 2015, the S&P 500 index averaged 9.85 per cent return per year, yet the average investor earned only 5.19 per cent. Why the difference? Behaviour. Investors traded – bought and sold – when they should have just left things alone. Selling when markets drop is the biggest destroyer of portfolio value.

During the COVID-19 pandemic, markets around the world fell by over 30 per cent within the space of a few weeks. Yet as I write, much of those falls have been recovered. Those who panicked and sold locked in losses that they didn't need to incur.

Markets will go up and down, and the down periods are normal. They're the risk – the reason you get that higher return that you are seeking. So be patient, and stick to your plan.

BORROWING TO BUY STOCKS

I find it puzzling that borrowing to invest in property is well accepted and relatively easy to do, yet borrowing to buy stocks is considered high risk and speculative. I had a client recently who's bought and sold numerous investment properties over the years, often borrowing 100 per cent of the purchase price, yet when I recently suggested that we put some of his surplus cash into a share portfolio and match his contribution with an equal amount of borrowings, so the portfolio was geared to 50 per cent, he baulked.

I find this puzzling because stocks are more liquid and far more easily diversified than property. The income from stocks is not dependent on a single tenant, and there are no ongoing costs. The difference stems from the fact that property is a physical asset – you can see it and touch it and that provides comfort. Property also has the perception of being more stable, because it's not valued every working day, as stocks are. The thinking goes that stock prices go up and down every day, therefore they are volatile, therefore they are risky.

Borrowing entails risk, of course – in fact, what borrowing does is magnify risk. Buy an asset with cash and it has a risk of X; borrow to buy the same asset and you get 2X risk, or maybe more. This is because, no matter what happens to the value of the asset that you bought, the loan must be repaid. Not only that, but throughout the life of the loan, interest repayments need to be paid, as a minimum.

However, risk and return go hand in hand. A strategy of little to no risk would take you to bank deposits, with returns typically lower than inflation. As illustrated by the doubling numbers earlier in this chapter, pushing your return up a percentage or two can have a significant impact in your long-term result. Using borrowings – 'leverage' or 'gearing' are other words to describe the same thing – is a way to take on extra risk to move your expected return up a few points. You are actively pursuing increased risk to access the higher potential return.

There are different ways to seek out increased risk in stock investment. Armed with your new understanding of the impact of compounding over time on the growth of your investments, let's say you decide you want to increase your level of risk from the standard broad stock-index level. One option is to leverage that broad index up through borrowings: perhaps you borrow an amount equal to the value of your initial portfolio. A second alternative to increase risk is to step away from the broad index and construct a portfolio that has less diversification and holds smaller, more speculative stocks. Here's a visual of the options:

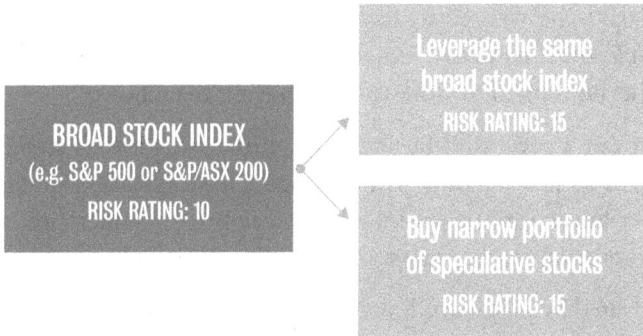

Both of these approaches will increase your risk and potential return. You just need to decide which risk you want to take.

I should mention that the 'risk rating' numbers in this diagram were just made up by me to illustrate the step up in risk. In practice, it's difficult to precisely quantify levels of risk, but not terribly difficult to recognise the different levels of risk between two options. An unleveraged portfolio will be lower risk than a leveraged version of the same portfolio; a narrowly diversified portfolio will be more risky than a broadly diversified one.

Want to dive deeper into stock market investment?

Our online course 'Invest in Shares with Confidence' can help you have a portfolio up and running in under 30 days. Find out more at www.financialautonomy.com.au/shares, and use the code BOOKVIP_STOCKS for $100 off the standard price.

Financial autonomy in action: The build

Clint and Leonie have been financial planning clients of mine for about 12 years. Right from the outset, Clint was clear about his goal – he wanted to have the choice of retiring at 50. He didn't know if he would actually want to retire when he arrived at 50, but he wanted to work towards having that choice.

Clint ran a successful business, so retiring was not as straightforward as just handing in his notice. He would need to either find a buyer for the business or develop a staff member who could take on management and allow him to step back.

Motivated by his goal, Clint avoided the common pitfall encountered by many of his business-owning peers: leasing an expensive car as a way to signal his success. Instead, he methodically built up his balance sheet. He bought premises to operate the business out of, then pushed hard to pay down the debt comfortably before his age 50 target. His thinking was that in retirement, the business would lease the premises from him, providing regular rental income.

Most impactfully, he bought stocks, both through his retirement fund and outside the regulated retirement system. He used gearing to magnify outcomes. We had a few different strategies over the years as his business grew, but as a minimum, several hundred dollars were added to his stock portfolios every month. Later on, that became thousands. He built and built, year upon year.

Along the way he put his two kids through school and enjoyed regular family holidays. Clint didn't pursue his goal at the expense of a full or happy life: he just wasn't wasteful and he kept his eyes on the prize.

When we caught up a year out from him turning 50, he was thinking he'd probably keep working a few more years yet.

Perhaps until his youngest child was through university, at least. He'd decided that his exit would be a sale – if he was out, he wanted to be completely out. There was no obvious buyer on the horizon, so he figured he'd keep going, ready should a sale opportunity arise.

I provided the numbers to show that his goal would be met – he was in a financial position to retire at 50 if he wished. He just needed a buyer.

Then, in a wonderful illustration of the maxim 'Good things happen to those who are prepared', a casual conversation with a friend in his industry revealed that this friend would be interested in buying Clint's business. Clint had an idea of what the business was worth: he wasn't greedy, but asked for a fair price, which the buyer could see was reasonable. It took about a year to get all the ducks in a row, but with a month to go in his 50th year, Clint was out.

While the proceeds from the business sale were an important piece of the puzzle in enabling him to achieve his goal, it still would have been impossible if he hadn't built up his investment assets year after year. Rent from the business premises forms an important part of his early retirement income, but the majority comes from his investment portfolio. This portfolio provides regular income via dividends, plus enormous flexibility in terms of access. Importantly, it's effortless from Clint's perspective. All he needs to do is pull together a few pieces of paperwork for his accountant at the end of the year – and even that is becoming increasingly redundant as online systems get linked together. Once he reaches age 60, drawings from his retirement savings portfolio will start to contribute to his income needs as well.

Clint unquestionably succeeded in gaining the choice in life that he sought. I'm looking forward to seeing what he dives into in the next chapter of his life.

GAINING CHOICE

Let's look at your financial autonomy action plan again. Are stocks a way forward to reach the goals you have recorded? Stocks are great, because you can start with small amounts and build over time. The cost to buy and sell them is minimal, and there are no costs to retain them. You can also sell them and get your cash quickly. They do, however, experience volatility, as discussed in chapter 4, making them unsuitable if your goals have shorter time frames.

PART FOUR
INVEST IN PROPERTY

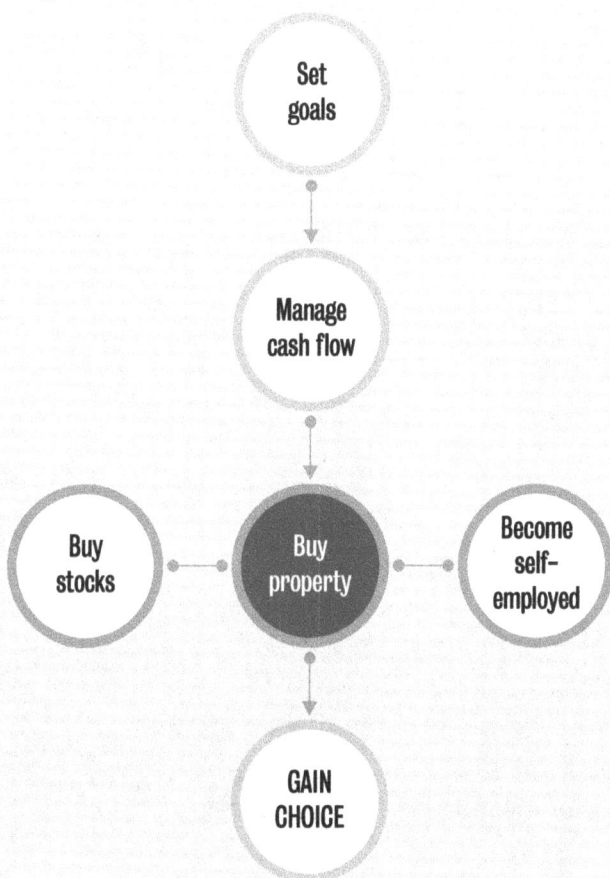

6

PROPERTY CASH FLOW AND DEBT

Before I jump in and start discussing how to choose properties to invest in, how many properties to buy and how to manage them, I want to talk about why you might buy property in the first place.

There are two main reasons:

1. Everyone needs somewhere to live.

2. You can use other people's money to leverage your returns.

One enabler to achieving financial autonomy and gaining choice is the generation of passive income – income that flows into your bank account without you needing to get out of bed. While it's not quite as passive as stocks, property investment certainly holds the potential to be a passive-income generator for you, providing regular and consistent income that typically keeps pace with inflation.

In most parts of the world, and certainly in Australia where I reside, investing in property without taking on debt is extraordinarily rare. The combination of high purchase prices, persistent growth in those prices (primarily due to a growing population) and minimal returns on cash saved in the bank means waiting until you can make an all-cash buy is not a winning approach.

Taking on debt, though, means taking on risk. The bank will always want its money back, no matter what unfolds. So, when embarking on a property investment strategy, it's essential that you have clarity about the money going in, the money going out, how those will balance, and plans for contingencies, such as the property being untenanted for a period of time.

MAKING MONEY INVESTING IN PROPERTY

As an investor, there are two ways you make money on your property. The first is by it rising in value over time. This tends to be where the big gains are made, but it's also the source of return that's least in your control. The second way property investors make money is the rent they collect from the tenant. This is far more predictable from the outset, when you purchase your investment.

As I mentioned, investing in property typically involves taking on debt, and debt needs to be repaid. The rental income produced by your property will be a very important piece in the puzzle when it comes to meeting your debt-repayment obligations. Depending on your long-term strategy, the rental income may also provide a passive income stream to gain you the choice in life that you're driving towards in pursuing financial autonomy.

When planning your property investment strategy, then, consider these two sources of investment return and how they might help you succeed. Let's look at the potential outcomes of each now.

Valuation-growth strategy outcomes

Upon the sale of your property, you hopefully have a larger sum than you started with. You could use this money to:

- live off for a period of time
- invest elsewhere, either in another or multiple properties, or in a different asset such as stocks
- top up your retirement savings.

Alternatively, a rise in your property's valuation could be used to grow your investment portfolio by accessing the equity that becomes available. Here's an example to illustrate:

Initial position	Five years later
Value of your property: $500,000	Value of your property: $600,000
Loan: $450,000	Loan: $450,000
Your equity: $50,000	Your equity: $150,000

The increased equity could be used to purchase another property. Let's assume your bank wants to see a 10 per cent deposit (equity) to approve finance, and you'd like to buy a second property, once again at the $500,000 price point:

New position (five years after original investment)	After second investment
Value of your property: $600,000	Value of property 1: $600,000 Value of property 2: $500,000
Loan: $450,000	Loan (over both properties): $950,000
Your equity: $150,000	Your equity: $150,000
Equity percentage: 25%	Equity percentage: 14%

As a result of your initial property investment increasing in value, your equity – the portion of the property you own after debt is repaid – has risen from $50,000 (your initial 10 per cent deposit) to $150,000. Consequently, your bank is willing to lend you 100 per cent of the purchase price on your next property, holding both properties as security, because with $150,000 of equity available, your total portfolio is still comfortably above the 10 per cent minimum equity the bank requires. (Note, banks may go as low as 5 per cent equity sometimes, but you should recognise that this is quite high risk – it wouldn't take much of a price downturn for all of your equity to evaporate.)

The benefit to you is that you now have exposure to the property market of $1.1 million, compared to $600,000 before the second purchase. If prices were to increase 10 per cent, your wealth would increase $110,000, whereas with one property it would only rise by $60,000.

This laddering approach – buying one property, leaving it for a period to grow, and then using the equity created to add another property to the portfolio – is a common property-investment strategy. It maximises the key advantage property has in the investment landscape: the fact that banks are happy to provide loans over property.

Rental-income strategy outcomes

Rental income is your regular cash flow and can be used to:

- assist with loan repayments – interest and perhaps principal
- provide an income stream once debt is repaid.

An important element in making property investment work is that over time the rent you charge should increase – by inflation as a minimum, but normally by a rate greater than that. Rent rises by more than inflation where the value of the property rises.

As the cost for someone to obtain a roof over their head goes up, it's logical that the rent required to live in a property that's now worth more will also be higher.

So your rental income rises, but importantly your loan repayments typically remain the same. They might vary with interest-rate changes, depending on your loan structure (which we'll talk about later in the chapter), but otherwise they'll remain stable. Here's how this rising rental income, combined with stable loan repayments, plays out over time:

Year	Monthly rental income	Monthly loan repayments	Cash-flow surplus/deficit
1	$1,000	$1,300	-$300
2	$1,040	$1,300	-$260
3	$1,082	$1,300	-$218
4	$1,125	$1,300	-$175
5	$1,170	$1,300	-$130
6	$1,217	$1,300	-$83
7	$1,265	$1,300	-$35
8	$1,316	$1,300	$16
9	$1,369	$1,300	$69
10	$1,423	$1,300	$123
11	$1,480	$1,300	$180
12	$1,539	$1,300	$239
13	$1,601	$1,300	$301
14	$1,665	$1,300	$365
15	$1,732	$1,300	$432
16	$1,801	$1,300	$501
17	$1,873	$1,300	$573
18	$1,948	$1,300	$648
19	$2,026	$1,300	$726
20	$2,107	$1,300	$807

Cash flow surplus/deficit

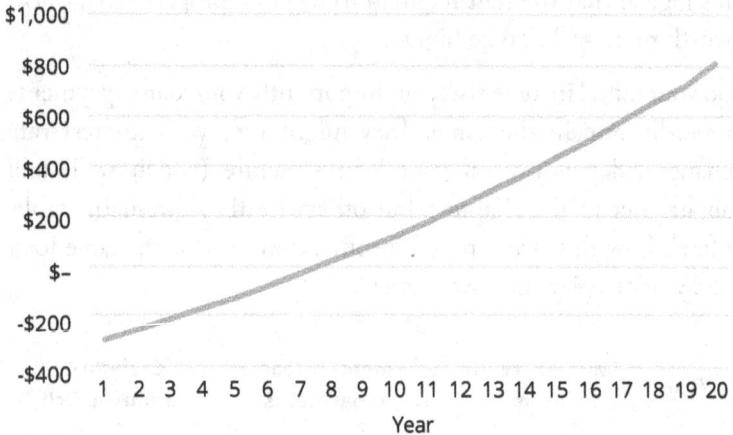

In the early years, loan repayments exceed your rental income. You will need to make up the difference. Give your property investment time, however, and eventually that equation flips, with rental income exceeding your loan repayments. Now you have positive cash flow, which you could use in any number of ways:

- Increase the loan repayments to pay off the loan quicker.

- Purchase another investment property or some other investment and use the surplus cash flow to help fund it.

- Use the surplus cash flow to help meet your living costs – a passive income source to help you gain choice.

I should mention that loan repayments are not your only outgoings as a property investor, of course – you also have expenses like council rates, insurance and maintenance. We'll cover those in more detail later in this chapter.

Damned lies and statistics

Property statistics are largely created by the property industry to help make them money. Every week, newspapers and the broader media will report that property prices went up by X per cent, or the median price in your suburb is now a squillion dollars. However, the numbers that sit behind these claims are super-rubbery. Take this example:

- I buy 123 Ricardo Street for $1 million.

- Five years later, I sell the property for $1.5 million.

- The newspaper and all the online records will report these numbers, showing a healthy $500,000 gain.

But:

- I paid $55,000 stamp duty to acquire the property.

- I paid $25,000 in agents' fees when I sold.

- I spent $300,000 on renovations and improvements.

- I contributed $24,000 of my own cash to cover the shortfall each month between rental income and outgoings.

So, far from making a $500,000 gain as the property statistics would tell you, my gain was actually a more modest $96,000. A huge difference. The poor quality of property growth statistics is a reason to put more focus on the cash flow of the property – that is far more transparent and verifiable.

BORROWING

By far the greatest investment attribute of investment property is the ease with which you can borrow to participate. I can't think of another investment asset where a bank will give you 80, 90 or even 100 per cent of the purchase price.

If I had a lump of cash to invest, say from a windfall, I'd generally put it into stocks, because owning stocks is effortless and has no ongoing costs. But if I had some surplus cash flow and a strong desire to build wealth, I'd be thinking about how I could use borrowing to propel me forward – and property is the asset of choice when it comes to borrowing to invest.

Borrowing can also be called 'gearing' or 'leveraging'. These two terms reflect the fact that borrowings enable a disproportionate outcome relative to the size of the initial investment. Here's a very simplified example of the power of gearing. I've ignored the interest expense of the loan here:

- Amount you have available for investment – $50,000

- Investment growth – 10 per cent

- Amount the bank will lend as a percentage of property value – 90 per cent

Scenario 1: Invest with no borrowings

Initial investment	$50,000
After 10% growth	$55,000
Profit	**$5,000**

Scenario 2: Invest with borrowings

Initial investment	$50,000
Amount borrowed	$450,000
Total invested	$500,000
After 10% growth	$550,000
Repay loan	–$450,000
Profit	**$50,000**

Again, this example is hugely simplified. The point I'm trying to illustrate is that by introducing borrowings into the investment strategy, the profit achieved is enormously enhanced. Of course, that cuts both ways. What if, instead of rising in value as we would hope, the investment declined in value by 10 per cent?

- Under scenario 1, with no borrowings, you would have lost $5,000.

- Under scenario 2, however, you would have lost your entire $50,000 investment.

Borrowing to invest amplifies your risk. Risk and return are opposite sides of the same coin: if you want strong returns, you must be prepared to accept the risk that is tied to that. You do, however, want to go in fully aware of the risks you're taking on, and with a plan as to how you can best manage those risks.

Here are five ways you can manage your risk when borrowing to invest in property:

1. Have a ten-year-plus time frame – property values go up and down, but historically, given long enough, they tend to rise.

2. Fix the interest rate on your loan so that a rising interest-rate environment won't force you to sell at a time when prices are depressed.

3. Run your initial numbers assuming that interest rates are 2 per cent higher than they are, so you know you can withstand higher rates should they occur.

4. Purchase a property for which the rental return covers most or all of the loan repayments, so if your circumstances change – for example, you lose your job – you won't be forced to sell.

5. Pay down the principal on your loan, so your equity position is progressively rising over time.

The power of gearing: my 68 per cent return

Way back in 1996, I bought my first home. It was a two-bedroom flat in a very ugly brown-brick building, probably built in the '70s with nothing done to it since. It wasn't flash, but it was within my budget and in a good location close to town. I paid $107,000. Now, I know that for those looking to buy their first home today, $107,000 is probably pretty sickening, but 20-odd years ago that was the going rate.

Four years later and I'd met the woman who is now my wife, and it was time to move from a flat to a house. We were starting to think about having a family. So I sold the flat for $189,000.

Those straight numbers – $107,000 purchase price, $189,000 sale price – look pretty good, right? They were. It equates to 15 per cent per year growth. But that 15 per cent doesn't tell the true picture. My actual return was just over 68 per cent per annum. Yep, you heard that right – 68 per cent!

When I bought my first home, I put down a 10 per cent deposit. So that meant I put in $10,700 and the bank funded the rest. There was some stamp duty, but it wasn't a lot at that price point, and I had a friend help me with the conveyancing so that cost me next to nothing.

Over the four years that I owned the flat, for much of the time I had a flatmate in the spare room, and her rent helped with the loan repayments. I didn't really make much of a dent in the loan during that four years, but it went down a little, and I had a roof over my head.

I sold for $189,000. The first thing to happen was that the associated loan needed to be repaid. With that done, I had around $93,000 in my bank account. Of course, I had to pay a real estate agent for the sale, and I had some legal costs. I can't recall exactly how much they were, but being conservative, let's say I was left with $87,000.

I bought my flat for $107,000, and sold it four years later for $189,000, a gain of about 15 per cent per year. But the real story here, the one relevant to me, is that I put down almost $11,000 of my savings, and four years later, that had become $87,000 – my savings had multiplied by a factor of eight!

While I'd love to say that I got this amazing return because I was some sort of property investment genius, the truth is it was pure luck. I bought when I could afford to buy, and I sold when I needed to sell. But you make your own luck. I wasn't to know the property value was going to increase that much, but by saving a deposit, finding something in my budget (even though it was a long way from being my dream home), and making a start, I enabled that luck to happen.

The power of gearing significantly magnified my outcome.

WHICH LOAN IS BEST?

There are two primary loan-structure decisions for you to make when taking out a property loan:

1. principal and interest vs interest-only repayments

2. variable interest rate vs fixed interest rate.

Let's look at these in more detail.

Principal and interest vs interest-only repayments

When you typically think of a loan, you imagine getting a lump sum from the lender, making regular repayments and then, one day in the distant future, the loan is paid off – zero. No more repayments needed. This is a principal and interest loan. With every repayment you make, you pay the loan interest plus a bit of the original loan amount – the principal. Early on, the amount that comes off the principal with each repayment is minimal, but this progressively changes, with more and more of each repayment chunking down your debt.

The alternative loan structure is interest only. The name is pretty self-explanatory here. All you pay is the interest on the loan: no principal. That means your loan never reduces. Stick to an interest-only loan and you will never pay it off. So why would anyone go interest-only? Don't you want to pay off your loan?

The logic is usually based on maximising exposure to the property market. If you can afford repayments of $2,000 per month (whether out of your cash flow or from rent), then with a principal and interest loan, you could borrow around $380,000. However, if you elect to have an interest-only structure, you could borrow $600,000. The interest-only loan thus enables you to buy more property, and if the value of the property rises, your gain is greater. Of course, if its value falls, you lose more, too.

Most loans over primary residences are principal and interest. We all want to own our home debt-free one day, so it makes sense to be progressively paying this down. Interest-only loans are used more often for investment properties, where people want to build a portfolio of multiple properties and therefore want to stretch their cash flow as much as possible. Having your loan as an interest-only structure might also stretch out the time your property is negatively geared, which may produce tax savings.

In deciding which structure is right for you in your journey to financial autonomy, you need to decide whether your strategy is to build a multi-property portfolio, on the basis you are bullish on rising property prices, or whether you're looking to property to generate passive income.

Under the first scenario (multi-property), you would likely favour the interest-only option, as this gives you maximum spending power and therefore maximum exposure to the property market. With the second, passive-income approach, you want to pay off the loan so that one day the rental income is yours to spend. Principal and interest repayments would therefore be the way to go, so that your loan gets lower and lower.

Variable vs fixed interest rates

A variable-interest-rate loan is a loan the interest rate of which changes over time. Central banks alter interest rates depending on the needs of the economy, and these changes flow through to retail banks. With a variable loan, as rates move, the interest rate applied to your loan moves. With a fixed-rate loan, by comparison, the interest rate that you pay is locked in for a period of time – usually somewhere between three and ten years.

In Australia, variable-rate loans are the most common; in the US, however, fixed-rate loans are the norm. So how do you decide which option is best for you?

Most people decide based on whether they're likely to save money through reduced interest costs by fixing their loan. Such calculations require you to 'guesstimate' where interest rates are headed several years in advance. These calculations are tough and, in truth, there's no way to accurately ascertain beforehand whether or not a fixed-rate loan will save you money in comparison to a variable-rate loan. You'll only know in hindsight.

A better approach to deciding between variable and fixed would be to assess the impact if interest rates were to rise. This is something you can do accurately. Between October 2009 and November 2010, interest rates rose 2 per cent, so let's use that as an example of what could happen in a rising-interest-rate environment.

If you have a $500,000 loan with an interest rate of 4 per cent, and it has 25 years to run, your monthly repayments will be $2,639 (with a principal and interest loan). If interest rates rose 2 per cent, your repayments would rise to $3,222. When deciding whether to fix your interest rate or not, the key thing to consider is whether such an increase will cause you financial distress. Is that extra $583 per month affordable? Fixing your interest rate should be thought of as insurance: you do it if, in your assessment, the consequence of doing nothing is potentially financially painful.

Over the years, I've had both types of loan. I've tended to lean more towards fixed loans on investments, as I've liked the certainty of knowing where I stand – I know the rent coming in, I know my loan obligations, and therefore I know what the shortfall is that I need to come up with.

Fixed loans tend to be less flexible, however, and that's another reason why they're typically less popular for your primary residence. There are often restrictions on making extra repayments, and changes mid-way through a fixed term will usually result in extra costs to you.

Especially on your primary residence, getting ahead on repayments is a really effective way to manage the risk of rising interest rates on a variable loan. When rates go up, the bank's computers will check whether you remain on track to have your loan cleared within the original loan term. If you've been paying more than the minimum for some time, then it's quite likely your loan will be well on track to being repaid within the loan term, even at the higher rates. You will not then be required to increase your regular loan repayments.

Savings vs debt

Here's something else for you to consider. Let's say you wanted to buy a property costing $500,000. Were you to save up the cash to make that purchase – not borrow any money – you'd need to earn somewhere between $700,000 and $950,000.

Why? Because to save, you first have to pay tax. If instead you use debt, you sidestep the tax issue. You get straight to the $500,000, only ever paying interest on this amount. You even get a tax deduction for that interest expense!

Building wealth through savings is tough (and slow). Provided you can manage the risk, building wealth through debt is easier. The low-interest-rate environment that the world is in at time of writing tips the scales even further in this direction.

THE COSTS OF BEING A PROPERTY INVESTOR

When it comes to your property-investment strategy, managing cash flow is foundational, as we covered earlier. Thus far in this chapter, we've focused on the loan repayments – they're certainly the largest of the outgoings, but are not the only expenses. Let's look at the other costs you need to allow for if you're an Australian investor.

Council rates and local taxes

Typically, council rates and local taxes come to $1,500 to $2,000 per year. This covers rubbish collection and provision of local facilities like libraries, parks and sporting grounds.

Land tax

In my state, and throughout Australia, a tax is payable by landlords based on the land they own. It's important to recognise that it's based only on the land value, not the total value of the property. As an illustration, if your investment property was worth $500,000 and the land value was assessed at $300,000, you would have $375 per year of land tax to pay. Own several properties with a combined land value of $1 million and you are looking at $2,975 per year.

Insurance

There are two insurances you need to prepare for as a property investor: landlords' insurance and building insurance. Landlords' insurance will typically cover loss of rent if a tenant breaks the lease, damage caused by the tenant or their guests, legal costs to evict a tenant and burglary. You can also get extra benefits such as cover for damage caused by pets. Building insurance covers your property for damage caused by fire, storm or flood.

The cost of insurance varies greatly depending on the location of the property and its value, but assume $1,000 per year for both coverages when developing your rough plan, and then get some quotes online as you narrow down your strategy.

Body corporate, owners corporation or strata fees

Apartments and units incur fees (levied by a body called an 'owners corporation', 'body corporate' or 'strata corporation' in different states in Australia) that cover maintenance and insurance for the building and/or common property areas. As a property investor, they can be a good way to gain reliability around maintenance costs, in that fees are (usually) payable quarterly and the money builds up in a pool, so that when works are needed, the funds are sitting there ready to go.

Again, such costs vary considerably depending on your property. Work on an assumption of $3,000 per year in your rough plans, and then refine this once you've done some shopping around.

If the apartment you're looking at has a pool, gym and lifts – double this fee.

Property-manager fees

You could choose to manage your investment property yourself, but most people engage a property manager to act as the go-between for you and the tenant. Property managers find a tenant for you, and then act as the contact person when the tenant has an issue. They will typically have a list of tradespeople too, so when works need doing, they can line things up for you. Their fees are usually in the range of 5 to 7 per cent of rent collected.

Utilities

Your tenant will be up for the costs of most utilities, but as the landlord, you may be responsible for water rates. Allow $400 per year for these.

Maintenance

Properties wear out – something property spruikers often gloss over. Carpets need replacing, dishwashers and hot water units come to the end of their life, fresh coats of paint are needed, and eventually there are big-ticket expenses like new kitchens and bathrooms.

The large expenses such as new kitchens would normally be funded by extending the loan on the property, so focus on having enough money available for the likes of a new hot water unit or air conditioner.

Vacancy periods

It's wonderful when a single tenant sticks around for years and years. You, the landlord, get stable, reliable income, usually with minimal fuss. In Australia, tenants stay put for four to five years on average. Inevitably, though, you will have a vacancy when one tenant leaves and it takes some time to get a new tenant. Often, during the changeover period, it might suit you to have the place vacant for a few weeks so you can perhaps apply a new coat of paint or do some other maintenance. You therefore need to ensure that from a cash-flow perspective, you can manage for a period with no rental income.

Accountancy fees

Accountancy fees are not a big cost: if you're a salary or wage earner at the time of writing in Australia, your annual tax return costs are likely less than $200 – if indeed you need to pay anyone to do your tax at all. Once you become a landlord, though, there is more to be done and so you need to expect your accountancy costs to rise. Allow for $300 per year and you should be quite safe.

YOUR PROPERTY-INVESTMENT CASH-FLOW PLAN

Now that you've identified the costs involved in being a landlord, let's work out your cash-flow plan. A blank version of the following table can be found in the companion workbook (www.financialautonomy.com.au/workbook). Note, personal taxes have not been allowed for here, as they vary enormously from person to person. Ensure that you include them as part of your plan, however.

From this analysis, if I'm to proceed with this property investment, I need to be able to afford $489 per month. I've been quite conservative, allowing for one month of rental vacancy and $1,200 per year for maintenance.

A sample cash-flow plan

	Monthly	Per year
Rental income	$1,600	$19,200
OUTGOINGS		
Loan repayments	$1,333	$15,996
Council rates and local taxes		$1,500
Land tax		$350
Insurance		$350
Body corporate/strata fees		$2,400
Property-manager fees		$1,152
Utilities		$220
Maintenance	$100	$1,200
Vacancy periods		$1,600
Accountancy fees		$300
TOTAL OUTGOINGS		**$25,068**
Cash-flow result		-$5,868
Monthly funding need		-$489

As discussed earlier in this chapter, over time you would expect rental income to rise, while expenses are likely to remain fairly stable, so your contribution should diminish. Nonetheless, prior to embarking on a property investment, it's essential that you run your numbers and ensure that you can afford it cash-flow-wise. Properties have high transaction costs and at best take several months to sell. You don't want to get into something and then discover six months or even two or three years later that you can't afford to keep it.

7

PROPERTY SELECTION
AND STRATEGY

Let's talk strategy, now. In order to determine if and how you can use property investment as a pathway to your goals, it's important to first think through the strategy options available. Keep at the front of your mind the goals you recorded in your financial autonomy action plan – these are your true north. Your strategy choices should be guided by the goals you're trying to reach.

I've identified five property strategy options for consideration, and in this chapter we'll explore the pros and cons of each, to enable you to identify the ideal strategy for your goals. I've created another short self-assessment tool to help you, too.

HOW MANY PROPERTIES?

Your first consideration is whether to build a portfolio of multiple properties with significant debt, or buy one property and focus on paying it off.

A multi-property strategy entails you making interest-only repayments on the associated loan of your first property, thus minimising your cash-flow outgoings. Once some equity has built up in the property, you use that equity (plus some savings if you have them) to buy a second property. Again, you pay interest only on the loan to minimise the cash-flow impact. Rinse and repeat as you're able.

What is equity?

Equity is the portion of the property you own. If you have a property worth $500,000 and you owe the bank $300,000, then your equity is $200,000 – the difference between the value of the property and what is owed on it.

The long-term aim of a multi-property approach is, at some point in the future, to sell off several of the properties and use the profits to clear all debts, so that you're left with one or more debt-free properties throwing off regular income.

The alternative is to focus on a single property and make principal and interest loan repayments so that your loan balance is reducing. As the rental income rises, you increase the loan repayments and work towards clearing the debt as soon as possible. This property then becomes a generator of passive income for you.

The appeal of the multi-property strategy is that you're diversified, both in terms of tenants and in the growth rates of individual properties.

The negative aspect is that you'll be carrying a lot of debt and, if there's a broad property downturn or interest rates rise meaningfully, you're potentially exposed.

In comparison, the single-property strategy represents less risk in terms of debt exposure, but you are totally reliant on the performance of this single property.

WHAT TYPE OF PROPERTY?

Next, you need to consider whether to focus on freestanding dwellings or go with apartments or units.

As a property investor, you hope that the value of your property rises over time. There are three types of potential buyers for your property, when the time comes:

1. owner-occupiers

2. investors

3. developers.

When considering the pros and cons of apartments versus houses, a key difference is that developer demand is likely to be non-existent in the apartment space. This means there's one less reason for your property to increase in value.

The upside to apartments, however, is that they will have a body corporate, owners corporation or strata corporation taking care of the maintenance and up-keep of the external elements of the property. This is significant. Houses require considerable maintenance to prevent them getting run-down and, if you have your own house to maintain and a life to live, you may not want the worry of maintaining an investment property too. Of course, you can pay people to do the work for you – most investors take this approach. Nonetheless, it all costs money and requires coordination.

To boil it down – apartments are less effort for you, the investor, but standalone properties usually have the potential for greater growth.

BIG CITIES OR REGIONAL TOWNS?

The third consideration is location. The higher number of people in big cities means that tenants are easier to find and properties are generally quicker to sell. However, property is much more expensive, meaning you need a larger deposit, a larger loan, or perhaps both. Regional towns have lower prices, making them more accessible and potentially allowing you to diversify your property portfolio. Loans can sometimes be harder to secure in smaller regional towns, though, as banks worry about being unable to sell the property should you default on your repayments.

RESIDENTIAL OR COMMERCIAL?

The default choice for most property investors is residential rather than commercial property, and there are good reasons for this. There's a lot more residential property than commercial property available, and banks offer more generous loans for residential properties – both in interest-rate terms and in the amount of deposit required. The key advantage of residential over commercial, however, is that vacancy periods are generally pretty short. With commercial properties, vacancies of many months are not uncommon, depending upon the location.

Despite these headwinds, commercial properties do offer some advantages. Once you have a tenant, they tend to be very 'sticky'. A business will fit out their premises, and if they have customer interaction, a portion of their goodwill is tied up in the physical place where they're trading. Your successful commercial tenants, therefore, are likely to want to stick around long term. Most leases are five years minimum, generally with several options for three- or five-year periods. It's not uncommon for commercial premises to be leased to the same tenant for ten-plus years.

The other nice thing about commercial property is that the tenant is responsible for everything. You only provide a shell – walls, roof and floor – and it's up to them to handle the rest, including expenses such as rates, water, power and body corporate. This means you have very low maintenance costs.

WHAT ABOUT RENOVATING?

The fifth consideration is whether or not you want to renovate. Are you a renovator looking to accelerate your wealth creation via some sweat equity, or do you want to be a passive landlord who only deals with the dollars and cents?

For those with renovation skills, property investment provides an avenue for you to build your wealth by putting in some hours and adding value to your investment. It's likely that a standalone house will provide greater scope for improvements, but freshening up the kitchen or bathroom of an apartment can deliver similar gains.

The renovator, therefore, is looking for the unloved property that needs some work. The passive landlord is chasing a property in good shape, ready to get onto the market.

DECIDE ON YOUR PROPERTY-INVESTMENT STRATEGY

Overleaf is a self-assessment tool to help you consider which property-investment options might best suit you and help you to achieve your financial autonomy goals.

Self-assessment: Which property-investment strategy is right for me?

Choose one option for each of the five questions.

1. Multi-property with high debt or single property with debt paydown?

   a) Multi-property if you are very positive about the outlook for property price growth, want to be an engaged investor, are happy to keep track of multiple properties and don't get stressed by high debt levels.

   b) Single property if you're more conservative (especially around debt), and your main aim is to generate a source of passive income as quickly as possible.

2. Freestanding property or apartment/unit?

   a) Freestanding houses if 1) you don't mind the maintenance, 2) they're not out of your price range and 3) you're keen to renovate and improve.

   b) Apartment or unit if you prefer a more passive investment, or you're looking for a lower price point.

3. Big cities or regional towns?

   a) Big cities if you want to minimise the risk of vacancy and have the ability to sell quickly.

   b) Regional towns if you're prepared to do considerable research to locate good-quality opportunities, or if your budget makes big-city property unaffordable.

4. Residential or commercial?

   a) Residential if you are looking to minimise risk and stick with something you're familiar with.

   b) Commercial if you're in a solid financial position and can handle periods of vacancy. It's helpful if you've been a commercial tenant before.

5. Renovator or passive landlord?
    a) Look for fixer-uppers if you have the skills, time and desire
        to renovate property.
    b) Choose a ready-to-rent property if you want to simply sit
        back and be a passive landlord.

* * *

Spend a few minutes now to determine the strategy that's likely to
suit you.

For my wife and I, our strategy is:

*   multi-property

*   apartments or units

*   big cities

*   residential property (primarily)

*   passive landlording.

PROPERTY SELECTION

So, once you've picked your overall strategy, how do you choose
the investment property that works for you? The starting point
normally is affordability, followed closely by comfort level.
Affordability comes down to how much cash-flow shortfall there
is and how much the bank will lend you.

Consider being conservative about what you spend on your
investment property, particularly if your strategy is to hold multiple properties. Faced with the choice of stretching myself and
buying a property for $700,000 or being more comfortable and
buying something smaller for $400,000, I'd choose the lower
priced option. I'd rather run with that for a few years and then
buy a second property once the numbers worked. That way, I'd

get two tenants paying income and two different properties, hopefully in different areas, diversifying my growth rates.

Do your research on properties. A growing population in the area where you plan to invest is very helpful, as there'll inevitably be rising tenant and owner-occupier demand. Also, remember that this isn't a house for you to live in! Just because a one-bedroom flat might not suit you doesn't mean it wouldn't make an excellent investment if the numbers stack up.

Avoid new estate and off-the-plan properties

I recommend that you avoid off-the-plan properties and properties on new estates. This will be controversial to some, but it's founded upon having witnessed the outcome of many property investments undertaken by clients I work with. My experience has been that investors who buy existing properties in well-established suburbs have tended to see the best results. Investors in new estates or those buying off the plan, by contrast, frequently seem to achieve negligible or negative returns for the first five to ten years. There are a few reasons for this:

- Price growth occurs when you have more demand than supply – buyers jostle for limited stock and bid the price up. In new estates and off-the-plan apartments, you have the opposite dynamic – lots of properties for sale, all looking for buyers.

- The price you pay for an off-the-plan or new-estate property includes the marketing commissions, meaning you're paying an inflated price relative to the value of the physical asset. Sometimes they offer things like rental guarantees, which further inflate the price.

- Just like when you buy a new car, you pay a premium for something that's fresh, new and looking its best. As an investor, this holds some appeal, in that it may be attractive for a prospective tenant – the first one, anyhow. However, just as that new-car smell doesn't last, neither will your property stay looking new for long. The short-term trajectory, then, is a drop in value – the exact opposite of what you're aiming to achieve.

- There are no valuation reference points. When you buy an established property, you can source data on similar properties that have sold in the area, and what they're renting for. But with a new development, and especially something not even built yet, how can you know what its true value is?

- You'll have competition for tenants. If a new apartment building goes up with 300 dwellings inside, it's a fair bet that at least half of those will be chasing a tenant. This doesn't give you much negotiating power as a landlord. Even once you get a tenant in, when you try to put the rent up $10 a week at the first renewal, there's a risk that the tenant will up and move down the hall, given the abundance of properties available for rent.

- Building defects. Whether it's dodgy plumbing, a leaking roof, tiles that come off or garage doors that don't work, new properties seem to have a lot of problems. Buy something existing and these irritants have already been ironed out for you.

I should acknowledge at this point that your accountant might have a different opinion on new versus old. They may argue that new is better because of the greater depreciation – a tax deduction. Having been in the investing game for over two decades, though, my observation is that making investment decisions based primarily on tax leads to poor outcomes. That's not to say the taxation elements should be totally ignored, just that they should be down the list several rungs, rather than being the key consideration when you're choosing between option A and option B.

What about location?

We're focusing on well-established suburbs, but how do we narrow the field further? Affordability, as I mentioned earlier, will be a starting point. If you have a budget of around $400,000, there's no point looking in suburbs where properties typically fetch $1 million.

Here are a few other factors you should consider:

- **population growth** – as increased demand must push up property prices

- **infrastructure** – access to public transport, freeways, green space and entertainment

- **jobs and industry** – people want to live close to where they work, so think about where your tenants might earn their living.

Population growth and property price appreciation

Japan has a shrinking population – between 2017 and 2050 it's forecast to reduce by a third. Fewer people, of course, mean lower housing demand and oversupply.

Between 1994 and 2014, ¥382 trillion was spent on residential construction, yet the total value of all residential property in Japan at the end of this period was only ¥357 trillion. That means the value ascribed to all the properties that existed before 1994 is zero, and even those more recently built are worth less than they cost.

Contrast this with the experience in China, where there has been mass migration from rural areas into the cities. In the eastern region of China, a 1 per cent increase in the population led to a 1.34 per cent rise in the value of properties (Lin et al., 'The Impact of Population Migration on Urban Housing Prices').

Rental yield

To invest in property, you'll (almost certainly) be borrowing funds – and when banks lend you money, they require you to pay it back. If you can structure your investment so that the rent your property brings in covers your loan repayments, or at least gets you close, then the burden on you to retain the property for the long term is greatly reduced.

Calculating the rental yield – that is, the property's annual rent divided by the property's value – is also helpful when comparing multiple properties. Consider this scenario:

- Property A costs $375,000 and generates rent of $1,560 per month.

- Property B costs $455,000 and generates rent of $1,840 per month.

Which is the better investment, purely on the basis of rental income? Let's look at the numbers.

Property A's rental yield

Yearly rent: $1,560 × 12 = $18,720

18,720 ÷ 375,000 = 4.99%

Property B's rental yield

Yearly rent: $1,840 × 12 = $22,080

22,080 ÷ 455,000 = 4.85%

The rental yield calculation tells us that, all else being equal, property A produces the higher return.

Rental yield is helpful when you're comparing multiple properties that have similar characteristics. It's less helpful when comparing properties in different regions or where the property type or condition is quite different. A property in inner-city Sydney, for instance, will almost certainly have a lower rental yield than a property in a small rural community, but this doesn't necessarily mean the property in the rural area is a better investment. As economic and population growth in big cities is typically higher than in rural areas, property value growth is likely to be higher. Investors are willing to accept a lower yield to get that growth. There are also more tenants available, so the risk of vacancy is far lower.

WHAT'S NEGATIVE GEARING ALL ABOUT?

Property investors in Australia hear a lot about negative gearing, so let's cover off what it is and why it matters. 'Negative gearing' refers to the situation where the rental income does not cover the full cost of owning a property – that is, the interest expense of the loan plus the other costs associated with holding the property.

If your property is negatively geared, from a cash-flow perspective it is losing money. For a negatively geared investment to make any sense, the value of the property needs to be rising at a rate faster than the cash-flow loss you are incurring.

On the surface, a negative-gearing scenario doesn't seem great. The reason it gets considerable focus is because the loss you incur is tax-deductible against your other income. People therefore rationalise, with partial justification, that since the loss they are making on the property reduces how much tax they have to pay, the ultimate cost of holding the property is not so onerous, and means the rate of growth required to make the whole endeavour worthwhile need not be unrealistically high. Of course, this depends on your personal tax situation. It's easier to make the numbers stack up if you're a higher-income-earner on a higher tax rate, since the amount of tax you'd save in a negative-gearing scenario would be greater. Conversely, if you pay no or little tax – say, because you're retired – then negative gearing is very unlikely to be a strategy worth pursuing.

As shown in the cash-flow table in chapter 6, investment properties commonly begin life negatively geared and then become positively geared over time – that is, the income becomes more than the outgoings.

Someone in a high tax bracket, perhaps with an aggressive investment approach, might choose to buy another property at around the time that their existing property will cross over into positive cash flow. That way, the cash-flow losses of the new property will keep their combined portfolio negatively geared, or at least neutrally geared. Others, though, will be quite happy to receive the extra cash flow their properties throw off. This money could be used for works on the property, for example, since your investment property is constantly wearing out – into a new kitchen or a fresh coat of paint. This reinvestment will help maximise the amount of rent you can charge, and is also likely to increase the value of your property.

Alternatively, the excess cash flow could be used for another investment purpose or to help fund your lifestyle. In the long run, owning an investment property or properties with positive cash flow is where you want to end up. That passive income is what will support you and give you the choice in life that is your goal.

OFFSET ACCOUNTS

If you have a mortgage that you want to pay down, and you have cash savings sitting in the bank, then chances are you should be using an offset bank account. Offset accounts are linked to your home loan, and the interest charged on your home loan is reduced by the amount sitting in the offset account. It looks like this:

Interest only charged on this amount

Home loan

Offset account

Say that your normal loan repayments are $2,500 per month, and of that, $2,000 is interest then $500 reduces the principal of your loan (i.e. is paying it off). If you had savings sitting in an offset account, the interest expense might reduce to $1,700. So now, with the same $2,500 repayment, you would have $800 going towards reducing your loan.

Roll this on for months and years and your loan will be repaid faster – and a debt-free home is a good thing to have when it comes to gaining choice.

Offset account vs extra repayments

So, why not just use your savings to pay off the home loan directly, instead of putting the money in an offset account?

Excellent question. Numerically, the outcome is the same. However, offset accounts are more flexible. Some home loans have minimum redraw requirements (e.g. $500), and they're just not built to operate as transaction accounts. Your offset account, by comparison, can be used to receive your wages or other income, pay your bills and hold your savings.

Offset accounts are really powerful in getting your loan paid off ahead of schedule. Give some thought to whether you can incorporate them into the cash-flow strategy you developed in Part Two of this book.

PROPERTY MANAGERS

As touched on in chapter 6, most investors will engage a property manager to find them a tenant and then manage that tenant relationship. Using a property manager provides a buffer between you and the tenant, ensuring you are not pestered by a difficult tenant or interrupted during your normal day job. Your property manager will chase the rent when it is overdue, and will make arrangements when any repairs are needed, drawing on the tradespeople they use regularly.

Using a property manager also allows you to invest in areas remote to you. Just because you live in one city doesn't mean you can't invest in property in a city ten hours away, if you assess that the investment is attractive.

Property managers, as I said earlier, typically charge between 5 per cent and 7 per cent of the rental income. A good property manager is worth their weight in gold, however, because they will find you a quality tenant who will respect your property and ensure that your asset is well maintained.

MANAGING THE RISKS

When I'm embarking on something big, I like to think of the four or five worst things that could happen and determine what I would do in those instances. If I can handle those scenarios, then I'm okay to move forward. So what are the worst-case scenarios in your property investment adventure? Here's my list:

1. Interest rates go up, pushing up my loan repayments.

2. The tenant leaves and it takes months to find a replacement.

3. The tenant trashes the place.

4. I lose my job and can't afford the difference between the rent on the one hand and the loan repayments and other running costs on the other.

Here's how I would manage each of these scenarios.

Interest rates go up

To manage the risk of interest rates going up, I'd get a loan that has a fixed interest rate for the first five years, so I have certainty over that period. By the time the fixed-interest period expires, the rent should have crept up a bit, and hopefully there'll have been some capital growth, so I'd have options: retain the property or sell.

Alternatively, before I made the decision to invest, I'd calculate what the loan repayments would be if interest rates rose by 2 per cent, and ensure I could still afford them without stress.

Tenant leaves and the place is empty

If the tenant leaves and my property is vacant, I'd drop the rent. I only buy in inner-city areas where there are always people looking for a roof over their head. So, if the property isn't getting let out, the price I'm asking must be too high.

Tenant trashes the place

Landlords' insurance provides protection against damage by a tenant, whether it's deliberate or accidental. (Landlords' insurance can also provide other benefits, such as covering loss of rent if a tenant breaks the lease – and it's tax-deductible!)

I lose my job

To manage the risk of losing my job at some point, I'd make sure I had cash savings to ensure the property could be retained for months, if not years, and I'd also ensure that the rent came as close as possible to covering the outgoings. Worst case, I'd just sell the property – even if I sell at a loss, the size of the loan isn't such that I'd lose my home or face bankruptcy.

To provide extra comfort, I'd put a bit extra into the investment-property bank account each month, so I had a nice buffer there in the event of something undesirable popping up.

OTHER THINGS TO CONSIDER

As I've said before, properties wear out – carpets need replacing, walls need painting and kitchens become dated. When developing your investment-property strategy, give some thought to how this will play out for you. Will you buy a property that's looking tired and do some improvements immediately upon acquisition? Or will you look to update the kitchen five or ten years down the track? Hopefully, over time the value of your property will rise, enabling you to increase your borrowings to fund bigger improvements.

I advocate having a separate bank account for your investment property – ideally an offset account. Have all of your rental income paid into this account and all the expenses come out of it. Calculate your cash-flow shortfall (chapter 6), and arrange an automatic transfer of this amount from your personal account into the investment property bank account.

Add an allowance for property maintenance, too, so that when an expense arises, you have the funds sitting there ready to go. (Note that in practice, the property manager will likely deduct the cost of repairs from your monthly rent. The extra you pay into the bank account will then plug the rental gap so your loan repayments are covered.) Also save enough money into the account to cover expenses if the property is vacant for a period upon changeover of a tenant. It will happen at some stage, and it's much better to have the cash sitting there.

Finally, don't ignore the transaction costs. A key negative of property investment compared to stocks is the very significant costs associated with getting in and, to a lesser extent, getting out. The big transaction cost in Australia is stamp duty – a tax levied when a property is transferred from one owner to another. Stamp duty on even a modest investment property will be around $20,000, and it can go up a long way from there. This cost should be added to your acquisition price to truly assess the success of your property investment. The way I think about it is that if I buy a $400,000 property and have to pay $20,000 in stamp duty to do so, then I'm under water until the property reaches a value of $420,000 – I've lost. I therefore need the property to grow in value by 5 per cent just to break even.

Other transaction costs include agents' fees (when selling), conveyancing or legal fees, loan-establishment fees, potentially fees for finding a tenant, and some adjustments to reflect ongoing property costs that the existing owner has paid in advance.

All these costs add weight to a key concept when investing in property – that it's a long-term investment.

Financial autonomy in action:
From roustabout to multi-property investor

John Pidgeon grew up on a sheep farm in Western Victoria and experienced just how hard life on the land can be. Weather extremes and volatile prices meant so much was out of his parents' control.

Property investment wasn't something John grew up with – all he knew about property was that it was barren and flat and you raised sheep on it. However, an uncle who was a retired bank manager got John thinking about property investment during his university years. The uncle observed that the wealthiest people he'd come into contact with during his career either owned businesses or were property investors. John liked the idea of owning something that he could see and touch, and he was drawn to the logic that housing is something people will always need.

John's uncle also planted an idea about property that was not the standard narrative we hear today. He advocated renting until you were at a point where you could buy your home outright, and in the meantime, investing in properties to build your wealth.

When John graduated from university and started teaching, he had enough income to make a small investment in rural Victoria, where property prices were more affordable than in the major cities. He and his sister put in about $3,000 each and borrowed the rest of the purchase price. They did some tidying up and simple improvements, then rented the place out. The rent was sufficient to cover the loan costs, so the property paid for itself.

A few years later, John decided he wanted to leave teaching and buy into a fitness business. The property had risen in value: in fact, it sold for roughly double the purchase price, and the profits enabled John to make his career change into fitness. Fuelled by this initial property-investment success, John was keen to re-enter the market as soon as his financial position allowed. He got into the Adelaide market, then expanded his portfolio into Melbourne, and later Sydney.

These days he lives on the beautiful Central Coast of New South Wales with his wife and three kids, coaching others on property investment and otherwise living off his property portfolio. He has the flexibility and freedom to be an active parent and pursue the things he's passionate about. He has certainly gained choice.

GAINING CHOICE

Refer back to your financial autonomy action plan. Does property investment look like the right strategy solution for achieving any of your goals? As we discussed, due to transaction costs involved, property is a long-term investment, so it fits best with long-term goals.

PART FIVE
SELF-EMPLOYMENT

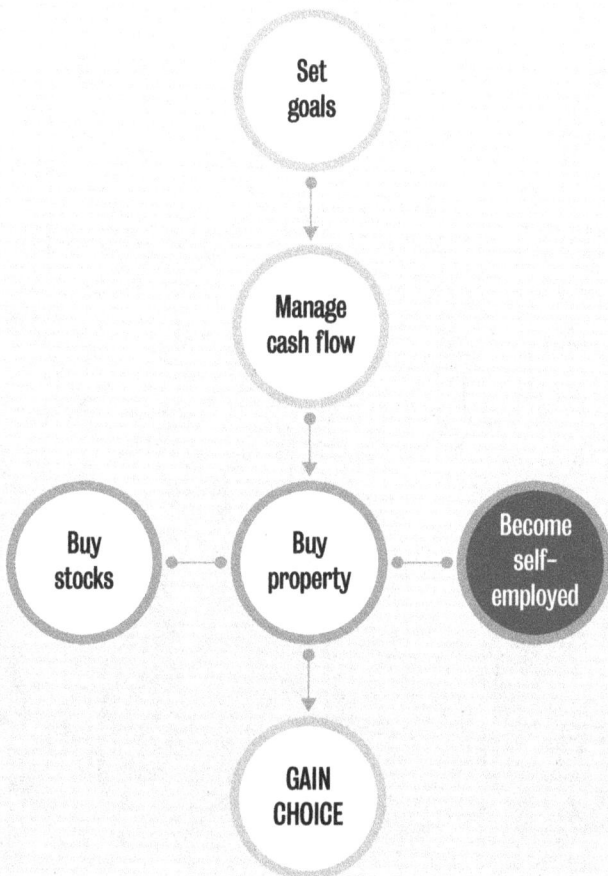

8

SIDE HUSTLES, IDEA VALIDATION AND STRATEGY

There's never been a better time than now to be self-employed. Internet-enabled tools allow us to collaborate, design, build and create to an extent never before possible (as highlighted unexpectedly during the COVID-19 pandemic). Also, whereas once, starting a business required enormous amounts of capital to build factories and warehouses, today multimillion-dollar businesses can be run on some laptops and a few monthly software subscriptions.

Self-employment is the primary way that I achieved financial autonomy and gained choice in life. In 2005, I left my role as a financial planner at one of Australia's largest banks and started out on my own. There were many challenges, among them buying a business which necessitated taking on an enormous debt, just as the global financial crisis hit.

I certainly have no regrets, however. Self-employment has enabled me to more fully participate in my children's lives when they were young – from classroom help, to basketball coaching, to school drop-offs and pick-ups. I've been able to pursue the things that interested me, like the idea of financial autonomy. As an employee I could never have devoted the time to building my podcast and writing this book. We've had six-week holidays, and once the kids are finished school, my wife and I have firm plans to spend two to three months each year living overseas and working remotely.

While I'm a very long way from being the next Warren Buffett, self-employment has also been more financially successful for me than remaining an employee. This is as it should be – self-employment entails risk, and you should be rewarded for taking on that risk.

In this chapter, we're going to start by looking at the idea of a side hustle. For many people who are planning a move to self-employment, a side hustle can be a useful way to make the transition that maximises the likelihood of success while minimising risk. We'll also consider strategy and framing an actionable business plan. Then, in the next chapter, we'll dig into pricing strategies, profit and other money stuff.

SIDE HUSTLES

When planning your pathway to financial autonomy via self-employment, an awareness of the concept of the side hustle is invaluable. Put simply, a side hustle is a low-risk method of undertaking an entrepreneurial pursuit. I'm aware that some would broaden the idea of a side hustle to include second jobs (umpiring football, Uber driving or working Friday nights at the local bottle shop, for example), but for our purposes here I'm going to limit the focus to business endeavours.

A macho 'burn the boats' approach to moving to self-employment is both imprudent and unnecessary in most cases. Using a side-hustle approach removes the need to quit your job on day one. However, the side-hustle approach to transitioning to self-employment doesn't suit everyone. If you're an architect, for instance, and you plan on leaving your current employer and starting your own architecture firm, then you may not be able to apply the side-hustle method, as it would conflict with your obligations to your employer. A side-hustle approach is best suited to situations where you want to move into an area different to your current employment.

A helpful way to think about a side hustle is as the entrepreneurial equivalent of a scientist's lab – a way to experiment and learn, where the consequence of failure won't be catastrophic. In fact, very often it's the failures that we learn the most from. James Dyson famously created 5,126 versions of his Dyson vacuum cleaner before finally being successful on the 5,127th attempt. He learnt from each version, getting closer and closer to success with each iteration.

Perhaps you won't need quite so many attempts before you find a model that works, but it is important that you go into your journey towards self-employment with an awareness that complete success with version 1 is improbable. Armed with this knowledge, you're not going to bet the house on version 1. A far wiser approach is the side-hustle method of testing out version 1 while you still have your day job, with a low level of investment. Put the idea in front of customers and get their feedback, then learn and evolve.

This utilises a concept known as 'lean startup methodology', developed by Eric Ries, which we'll explore more shortly.

Financial autonomy in action:
A well-developed eye provides a side-hustle opportunity

Let's take a look at a side hustle that was rolled out by a friend of mine, Andrew. Andrew and his wife Andrea have always been interested in collectable antiques, particularly from the Art Deco era. They love going to auctions and scouring the internet for interesting pieces and had built up a bit of a collection. His office has fantastic antique posters, and their home has many lovely items.

Andrew and Andrea both work in traditional office-type jobs, and with two girls to raise, the antiques were only a hobby for a long time. In 2019, though, they came across an opportunity in a town not too far from them to rent floor space in a new antiques store. For $200 per month, they'd get a 3 metre by 3 metre space, and the shop owner would retain 6 per cent of sales.

They jumped at the chance to try their hand at some antique dealing, all the while continuing in their normal day jobs. Sales flowed almost immediately, with their pieces being recognised for their quality. Andrew and Andrea identified certain items that sold well and hunted down more of those, often buying from overseas sellers and bringing something rare into the local market.

At time of writing, I understand that all sales are being recycled into new stock, but Andrew loves hunting for new items, and the fact that he can now pursue that passion 'guilt-free' is fantastic. They recently opened an online store on Etsy, MRMantiques, and will be pushing hard into antique fairs later in the year.

Andrew's brain is certainly ticking over about when this venture could replace at least one of their wages. Every time a piece sells, it's a minor victory, confirming they were right in seeing the beauty in that item and being prepared to back themselves. They've already run the numbers on the capital requirements of stocking a full store (it's a lot). This is incredibly valuable information that they'd have had little gauge on if they hadn't first embarked on this side hustle.

It may be that this business is only ever a side hustle, and for Andrew and Andrea that would be fine – they can enjoy the search for interesting items and make a few dollars along the way as pieces turn over. However, I wouldn't be at all surprised if, five or ten years down the track, when their kids are older and their personal balance sheet is robust, Andrew doesn't give away his current role and spend his days trading antiques full time. Maybe it won't make them rich (though maybe it will, who knows), but importantly, he'll be having a ball – he will have gained choice.

Sometimes your side hustle reveals that your business idea just plain sucks. Many years ago, two friends from university and I started a business offering an offsite backup service. This was before the days of Dropbox and the like. Backups at the time, if done at all, were done manually to physical disks. We identified some software that would allow us to provide the service and hired a sales guy to get out and see if he could win some customers. We didn't get a single customer, the sales guy quit, and the whole thing came to zero.

Fortunately, though, none of us had given up our day jobs, and we didn't lose enough money to do any of us significant harm. We'd lost time, but we gained plenty of insights, and I don't think any of us regretted giving the idea a go.

A side note on side hustles

In this section, I'm exploring the use of side hustles as a pathway to self-employment. Side hustles, however, could also be used to help you achieve financial autonomy even if you never intend to give up your regular job.

Perhaps you develop a side hustle refurbishing old gym equipment on the weekend. You buy the equipment from hotels that regularly upgrade theirs, replace the belts and other areas that show wear and tear, and then sell them on eBay and the like. You enjoy tinkering in the garage doing these machines up, and you spend one night a week loading up new stock online and handling sales queries.

Yes, this is an idea I've seen someone implement very successfully. This side hustle throws off around $2,000 profit most months: enough to cover an annual family holiday and build up a stock portfolio. It also provides a welcome second income stream for their household, taking a little pressure off the couple's primary incomes.

Bottom line: starting a side hustle that's intended to remain a side hustle is totally fine and can prove extremely useful for gaining choice. Check out my interview with Anna Stroud, podcast episode 138, for another excellent example.

IDEA VALIDATION

Often, a key hurdle for people making the move towards self-employment is finding an idea that feels right. Having read about, spoken to and interviewed many, many people about side hustles and transitioning to self-employment, I can let you in on a little secret – there's never a perfect idea!

As I touched on earlier with the Dyson vacuum example, the first version of your idea will not be the final thing that works in 99 per cent of cases. Airbnb is a huge success now, for example, but originally it was just two guys trying to earn extra dollars by renting out some air mattresses on the floor of their apartment when a big conference was in town. After that initial, very small success, they worked on a flatmate matching service. It bombed. They persisted, however, relaunching the Airbnb concept at least four times, with the advantage that the minimal traction from previous efforts meant that no-one noticed they were launching something that had been launched before. It took them time to figure out what would work.

The point here is not to get fixated on having one, brilliant, 'reshape the world' idea. If that's the hurdle you set yourself, you'll get nowhere. You'll procrastinate and never start anything. Instead, start something – really anything – and learn from it.

Here are some of the things you'll learn from starting a side hustle:

- whether you actually enjoy doing this thing
- whether the industry is interesting
- how to attract customers – and a tonne of ways that don't work!
- what price people are prepared to pay for your product or service
- digital and social-media marketing
- bookkeeping
- cash-flow management
- how to negotiate
- branding
- networking.

I'm sure there are plenty more. All this learning means that even if you start a side hustle and six months later wind it up completely, it's still not a failure – you've gained an incredible amount of knowledge that no textbook could ever teach you. I've no idea who originally said it, I've certainly found it to be true that 'The best ideas aren't evident until you're in motion'.

So the bottom line – get out there and have a go!

A great way to get started is to apply the approach outlined by Eric Ries in his excellent book *The Lean Startup*. First, you develop what he terms a 'minimum viable product' – it's not the fully fledged offering that you eventually want to sell, but it's sufficient for you to test your idea and see if people are willing to hand over actual money. Don't miss the 'viable' part here. A rubbish product won't give you an accurate indication of whether your idea will fly.

Build the best offering you can, maybe just keep it quite narrow in terms of the problem that it solves. For example, you might plan on creating a full clothing range for kids under age five. Your minimum viable product, though, might be girls' clothes in sizes 1 to 3. That's enough to establish whether buyers like your designs, if you can sell them at a price that makes the idea viable, and whether you actually enjoy doing it.

Here's a visual to illustrate the basic concept:

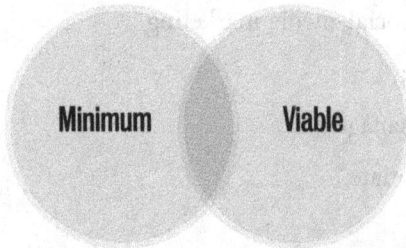

Minimum   Viable

The key value you derive from this initial product is that you *learn*. You learn if anyone is prepared to hand over real money for your idea. You learn through the feedback of both those who bought and those who didn't. Maybe the product was good but the price was wrong. Perhaps your target market didn't understand what problem your offering would solve for them. Your pathway forward is as follows:

- evaluate – what worked, what didn't?

- learn – what do you now know that you didn't know previously?

- modify – how can you improve what you're offering?

Applying this approach removes the tendency to delay and procrastinate on starting a side hustle until you have the perfect idea. Instead, you're merely embarking on a project to test out an idea and learn from it. Testing could be as easy as running some Facebook ads and seeing what sort of response you get. Indeed, if you're a little bold, you could run a campaign promoting a product you haven't even created yet and, then if you get some take-up, you can get cracking and build it. Kickstarter campaigns use this approach to great effect.

Before I move on from discussing idea validation, I think it's also worth mentioning that the saying, 'Imitation is the sincerest form of flattery' is apt here. If you see an idea that someone else is doing and think you can do it better, go for it. Google wasn't the first company to build a search engine, Microsoft didn't invent the spreadsheet or the word processor, and Enzo Ferrari wasn't the first person to attach four wheels to an engine.

Your idea doesn't need to be sexy, either. Plenty of people have built successful businesses cleaning offices at night, or putting together IKEA furniture for people who can't face doing it themselves. Boring can be just fine, so long as you find it enjoyable.

Financial autonomy in action: Parlaying career experience into a successful side hustle

Ruby Lee (whom I interviewed in episode 22 of the podcast) started her working life in accountancy. She'd completed university and gotten into a well-respected firm. She was making good money and, to those around her, the impression was she was out of the starting blocks and powering along in her chosen career. The problem was, she'd come to realise accountancy wasn't for her.

It took 18 months for Ruby to extricate herself from accounting and start her professional life over, this time in human resources and recruiting. Over the next ten years, she gained experience at various large corporates, building teams. At the time of our interview, she was working for a company that helps tech start-ups grow and scale, with Ruby responsible for building the teams necessary to make this growth happen.

Ruby's professional journey, and her experience in working with employers and job-seekers, led to her being something of a go-to resource within her network for all things career-related. During a period of maternity leave, she took the opportunity to start a blog, as a way to establish a library of content for her ideas and learnings. She was driven by the twofold desire to help more people and to build a second income stream.

The Career Emporium was born. Ruby developed a YouTube channel and offered one-on-one career coaching. As the business grew, she experimented with different online courses and group coaching to magnify her impact. Through this, she learned about the challenges and obstacles people were facing and was able to refine her offering to address the specific pain points of her growing community. Not everything she tried worked: her side hustle provided a real-life testing laboratory for her ideas.

By 2018, Ruby had reached the point where she wanted to go all-in on her business, resigning from her day job and turning her side hustle into her full-time gig. Ruby's business has evolved since, with an increased focus on entrepreneurship. These days, Ruby has flexibility and an ability to earn a living immersing herself in her area of passion. She's even gotten a TV gig on Amazon Prime!

SELF-EMPLOYMENT STRATEGY

Let's say that you've determined that you want to pursue the self-employment pathway to get you to your financial autonomy goal. You've found an idea that is worthy of testing. So, how do you move forward?

You need a strategy.

Now, I've said that your first idea is highly unlikely to create the full success story of your dreams, and that you're almost certainly going to need to adapt and evolve your idea as you progress. So spending weeks or months building out a detailed 50-page business plan to flesh out your strategy is weeks or months of wasted time.

Here's the solution, my one-page business plan. Work through the five questions either here or in your workbook (financialautonomy. com.au/workbook) and you'll have taken the first step to starting your side hustle.

One-page business plan

1. What problem will your business solve, and for whom?

2. How will people learn about what you're offering?

3. The dollars. What will it cost to deliver your product or service?

4. What does success look like? Quantify it.

5. What are the three critical things that need to occur for you to go ahead and become successful?

Next actions

- Consider pricing, building out from your answers to 3 and 4.

- Create a marketing plan, building out from point 2.

It may only be one page, but don't be surprised if some of these questions require you to step back and do some heavy thinking. Let's explore each of the five aspects in more detail now.

1. What problem will your business solve, and for whom?

Let's say you plan on making a gym bag for women. What problem will your gym bag solve? What's wrong with the bags that are currently out there? What do women need in a gym bag that isn't currently being provided?

Next, of course, who is your target market? Obviously in this case it's women who go to the gym, so that's an excellent start, but you could narrow it down still further. Is it for women who want to go to the gym before or after work, or for mums who need to drop their toddlers at crèche along the way? These different target audiences will have different needs, and certainly the marketing solution to get your product in front of each of these potential customers will differ.

A good process to help you get clear about what problem you'll solve, and for whom, is to ask your social-media connections to answer a simple questionnaire. Free tools like SurveyMonkey can enable you to gain clarity and test your assumptions. Ideally, ask your friends to share the survey around as well, so you get a wide variety of responses. The insights you gain could save you many, many hours, and plenty of dollars, too.

2. How will people learn about what you're offering?

In my experience, how people will learn about your prospective offering is the bit most easily ignored or brushed over. It's so easy to get caught up in the excitement of your idea and just assume that once you put it out into the world, people will be breaking down your door to hand their money to you.

Sadly, business rarely works that way. Consumers are generally wary of new products – no-one wants to be first – and however beautiful your new website is, it's one of about three million new websites launched that day. The cliché is 'a drop in the ocean', but when it comes to the internet, even a single drop is probably generous.

The foundation here is your answer to question 1 – being clear about who your product is for. (For clarity, when I say 'product', it need not be a physical product: it could equally be a service. I mean 'product' in a broad sense – your offering, whatever that is.) How will you reach that target market? Word of mouth, a local farmers market, social-media promotion, flyers in people's letterboxes? There are plenty of possibilities, each with their pros and cons.

In your one-page business plan, write down some ideas that make sense. You can flesh these out into a marketing plan, if you wish. Just recognise that this is super-important to your success – don't skim past it. You might have the best product around, but if consumers don't know about it or just don't care, you won't be in business very long.

This is an area where you can call in the help of friends and family. It's super-easy for those who love you to share your new endeavour via social media, so don't be afraid to ask. Your marketing budget isn't huge, after all. Embracing the 'hustle' is all-important when it comes to getting the word out to your target audience.

Establishing an origin story

Pro tip. I came across a great idea in Chris Guillebeau's succinctly named book *Side Hustle*. He suggests establishing an 'origin story' for your business endeavour. He used the example of a newly married couple who started a side hustle importing cashmere clothing from Nepal and selling it into their local Canadian market. Now, they could have described their business along these very factual lines, but that wouldn't have got much social-media traction, let alone traditional media coverage, nor would it have motivated people to give their products a try.

Instead, they told an origin story. They explained that the wife in this couple was originally from Nepal, and that they'd travelled to Nepal for their honeymoon and came across these great cashmere products. They recognised how well suited these fabrics, made for the harsh cold, would be to Canadian conditions. They also recognised that many of the farmers who produced the raw materials were poor and struggled to pay for the education of their children, with young girls being disproportionately impacted. To help address this, they undertook to donate 5 per cent of all profits back to charities in Nepal that focused on childhood education, especially for girls.

Armed with this origin story, they were able to get coverage in the fashion section of their local tabloid, and that exposure helped ensure that their initial shipment sold quickly and with a healthy profit margin.

An origin story could have so many uses – on your website, in press releases, promotional material, product packaging. It's certainly an idea worth considering when planning your business launch.

3. The dollars. What will it cost to deliver your product or service?

What do you need to charge to make your idea a viable business? Beware of the common trap of underpricing your offering! The temptation is to set a low price to make it easy to get sales early on – to win customers by being cheap. You need to ensure you charge enough, so that you can invest back in the business to fuel growth.

I've seen plenty of small businesses fade into oblivion, not because there were no customers or sales, but because the owner just wasn't making enough profit to enable growth and sustainability. Your interest in your business will wane quickly if it becomes a form of modern-day slavery.

We'll explore pricing more in the next chapter.

4. What does success look like?

Use the classic 'start with the end in mind' approach. Be clear at the outset what your goal for the business is – is it to earn some extra cash to pay off the mortgage or cover an annual holiday? Perhaps it's to build a business that will enable you to one day quit your current job. Whatever your definition of success is, put some numbers around it. Success, to you, might be earning an extra $2,000 a month, or being able to leave your current job in twelve months. Always quantify.

Having clarity in this area can help you avoid the pitfall of saying yes to everyone. There's a great quote I've put up in my wardrobe: 'You can do anything, but you can't do everything'. Ensure that, as you develop your business, each decision you make gets you closer to the success that you define in this step.

5. What are three things absolutely critical to your success?

Finally, ask yourself, what are the three most crucial prerequisites for success in your new venture, and how can you make them happen? These questions are often missing from business-plan templates. Procrastination can kill a move to self-employment, and it's often fuelled by overwhelm – having so many things to do and not knowing where to start.

So, identify three things that need to happen if this idea of yours is to bear fruit. Using the gym-bag idea mentioned earlier as an example, the three things could be:

1. creating a bag prototype
2. finding a manufacturer
3. selling at least ten bags to people outside of your family and friends within a month of your initial product run arriving.

If these things aren't achieved, your idea will shrivel up and die. Make your list and focus on ticking these things off!

Three important final points

Before we move on, here are three important points to remember as you write your one-page business plan and get started with your new venture:

1. Don't forget: 'Evaluate – Learn – Modify'. Always be learning and expect your idea to evolve as you do.

2. The idea is the easy bit – success comes from the execution. Be prepared to do the work.

3. Don't be too locked into your plan. You have a key advantage over large companies – nimbleness. If a great opportunity pops up, embrace it, even if it wasn't what you'd planned on doing this week or month.

Financial autonomy in action (1): From project manager to author

There's a common perception that people are either creative, or they're good with facts and figures: never both. Joanna Penn, who I interviewed in episode 81 of the Financial Autonomy podcast, illustrates just how wrong that thinking can be.

Joanna had quite a journey to financial autonomy. From university, she went into management consultancy, which is high-paying but comes with gruelling demands. Periodically she would quit a role and pursue other interests. She did some travelling, but also started several businesses – a scuba-diving company in New Zealand and a property-investment business in Queensland that bought, renovated and then sold properties. After each endeavour, she would return to her 'day job'.

She came to the realisation, however, that a side hustle would be a better approach. Rather than resigning each time she wanted to try out an idea, she would hang onto the Monday-to-Friday job and pursue her idea on the side.

Another important realisation came in 2008, when the GFC hit. Joanna was laid off and immediately saw how vulnerable she was: her life was held together by a single source of income and, when it was turned off, she was in a dire situation. Fortunately she was re-hired three months later, but she returned with a new attitude.

She'd fulfil the requirements of her role, but pursuing a career path was no longer in her plan. Instead, she viewed her job as a short-term enabler of building her own business, with multiple sources of income so that she'd never again be exposed to the whims of an employer or experience the vulnerability of having her life rely on a single source of funding.

Joanna started writing fiction and non-fiction, publishing books and creating a blog. In 2011, she was able to quit traditional employment entirely, and by 2015 she was earning more in her own business than she used to as an employee.

Her business continues to grow and, when we spoke in 2019, it was at the point where her husband was going to resign from his senior-management role to work with her. She hadn't reached seven figures, income-wise, but it seemed that wasn't far away.

Financial autonomy in action (2): Using online marketplaces to scale a business

It's not necessary to reinvent the wheel when it comes to building your side hustle. In fact, given that the idea is to keep your day job, at least at the outset, using existing infrastructure and systems can be a very wise strategy.

In episode 28 of the Financial Autonomy podcast, former mechanical engineer John Cavendish shared how he's gained the choice in life he was after by building a business on Amazon using their Fulfillment By Amazon (FBA) service. FBA allows entrepreneurs to run shops on their platform, without the need for warehouses or logistics. You simply send your products to Amazon, they store them in their warehouse and, when someone buys, Amazon handles the delivery.

John started with an initial investment of £5,000, spent mainly on inventory. Within 13 months, he was turning over £50,000 a month, and that rapidly grew to more than £100,000 per month. He got to this level with just one remote employee, highlighting the value of using existing marketplaces and, in this case, the services provided via FBA to grow a business without needing to invest unacceptable amounts of his time and money.

These days, John splits his year: living in Europe through the middle of the year but escaping to somewhere warmer when it turns cold. When I spoke with him for the podcast, he was in Ho Chi Minh City, Vietnam.

9

PRICING, PROFIT AND
MONEY STUFF

In the previous chapter, we explored how to use a side-hustle approach to move towards self-employment in a low-risk fashion. We discussed breaking through the idea barrier and developed a concise strategy to help roll out a self-employment plan.

In this chapter, we get into the nitty-gritty of dollars and cents. If self-employment is a pathway you choose to follow in your journey to financial autonomy, I want you to be aware of the trap many self-employed people fall into – working twice as hard as they used to as an employee, for half as much money.

This usually happens when you're a great technician and invest a tonne of time into producing quality work that you're proud of, but don't charge what you should. It can also happen because you feel you need to price low to win business. In addition, it can be the result of wearing many hats – including practitioner, salesperson, finance manager, head of marketing, bookkeeper and chief strategy officer.

Let's cover a bit of business 101 to help you avoid this Bermuda Triangle, and dig into pricing, profit and money stuff. First, though, I want to discuss the financial autonomy hierarchy of needs for people pursuing self-employment.

THE FINANCIAL AUTONOMY HIERARCHY OF NEEDS

At some point you've probably come across Maslow's hierarchy of needs. It's a framework to describe human motivation that has weathered the test of time well. Take a look:

Maslow's hierarchy of needs

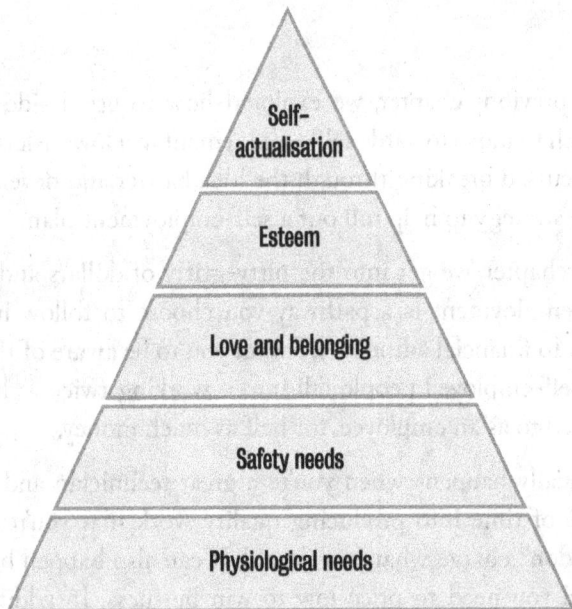

- Self-actualisation
- Esteem
- Love and belonging
- Safety needs
- Physiological needs

A key assertion in Maslow's framework is that you can't progress to the higher levels until you've achieved the lower levels. You build from the base up. There's no point worrying about love and belonging, for instance, if you don't at least have your physiological needs covered – air, food, water and shelter.

This approach is useful in planning your move to self-employment. There's so much wisdom offered when it comes to building and running a business – from marketing, to outsourcing, to leadership – that's it's easy to focus time and energy on higher-level things before you've got your foundations well established.

Here's my financial autonomy hierarchy of needs for those pursuing self-employment:

The financial autonomy hierarchy

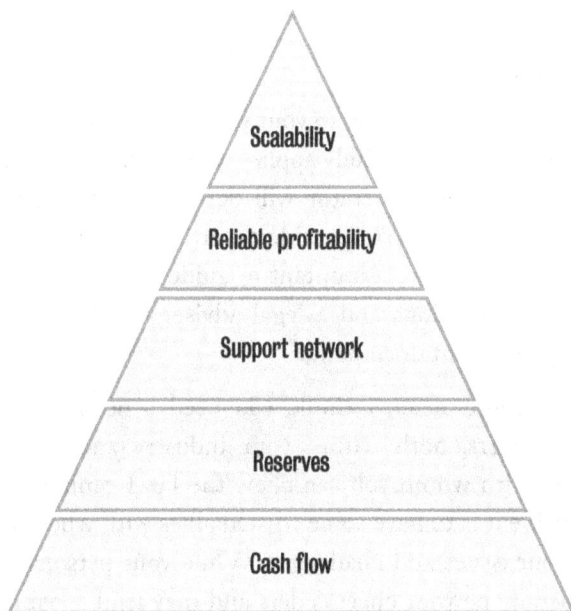

Scalability

Reliable profitability

Support network

Reserves

Cash flow

Cash flow

At the base is cash flow. This is the 'physiological need' of any business (and of any financial-autonomy goal too – thus chapters 2 and 3). If you don't have money coming in, you don't have a business.

Reserves

With that achieved, you look to build reserves: financial capital to provide the security that you need so your business can survive beyond the short term. For most businesses, cash flow is lumpy – cash reserves are essential to be able to ride out the normal peaks and lulls that all businesses face. Progressing to the higher levels without first building reserves could see your business collapse at the first moment of adversity. Reserves provide resilience for your business.

Support network

From reserves, you move up to your support network. The phrase 'no man is an island' definitely applies to running a business. Your success as a business operator will depend on the network of people you can build up to provide expertise or labour where you need it. You'll need an accountant to guide you on your tax and compliance obligations and a legal adviser to review contracts and draft important documents.

Most important of all, I think, you need a network of other business owners, both within your industry and from other industries, with whom you can chew the fat. I cannot overstate how valuable it is to have some trusted allies with whom you can discuss your issues and challenges. While your personal friends will hopefully be your cheerleaders and may lend a sympathetic ear, they most probably won't be self-employed. Someone who's never experienced the worry of intermittent cash flows, sporadic new client leads or a difficult but financially important customer simply can't offer useful advice to help you move forward. You need people in your network who are self-employed and running businesses.

Over the years, your support network will grow organically. Initially, it might be made up of former colleagues. If any of these leave their job to become self-employed before you, make it a priority to buy them lunch and learn about their experience. You might also connect with others in your field through professional associations or conferences.

A key reason many people decide to base themselves in a co-working space is to have other entrepreneurial people around them. These fellow entrepreneurs can provide the sort of fresh ideas and energy they need to push through the challenges that all business owners face.

Reliable profitability

With your support network in place, your next move up is to reliable profitability. Like any business, some months will be more profitable than others, but you reach a point where you're confident of your business being profitable in the short and medium term. Perhaps you have clients on contracts that pay you reliable monthly income, for instance. Or maybe your volume of sales is such that, even though individual customers change and there's some natural seasonality, there's a high level of predictability to your revenue and profits.

Reaching this level in the hierarchy is a major milestone in your business. With reliable profitability you're able to hire staff, commit to a lease for premises and invest in areas like branding and training. In many ways, reaching reliable profitability is the definition of success as a self-employed person.

Scalability

While reliable profitability is indeed an achievement you should take great pride in, there's one more level you can pursue – scalability. At face value, this means growing the business, but the real significance of achieving scalability is that the growth can happen without you, the owner, being 'on the tools'. The scalability phase could be considered a metamorphosis, just like a caterpillar becoming a butterfly. You move from being self-employed to being a business owner.

Strong, repeatable systems are at the core of this transformation. There's only one of you, and if you remain essential to the successful daily functioning of your business, then you've built yourself a prison. Maybe it's a prison in which you can spend money on nice things, but if you can't take a few months off to travel, or to spend time with a sick relative, then you haven't succeeded to the fullest extent on your self-employment journey.

I'm ascending to this final level in my financial-planning business as I write these words. I've built the business to have three very skilled team members, and I have the reliability of profits to be confident that I can pay their wages while also providing for my family. The team is capable of running the business in my absence; however, at present I'm the only licensed adviser in the practice. So unless I'm in the office, no new clients can come on board and no large changes can be made to existing client arrangements.

Achieving scalability is hard, which is why it's at the top of the self-employment hierarchy. Plenty of small businesses never achieve it.

Sometimes, though, I come across newly self-employed people who are working on the scalability objective from day one. I'm all for building good systems and processes early and embedding them in your business – systems provide the foundations for scalability in the future. However, I encourage you to recognise that before you can truly execute on this piece, you first need to have achieved the other stages. Produce cash flow, as without it, you have no business. Build reserves, so your business doesn't collapse at the first hurdle. Have a support network so you can leverage the wisdom and experience of others. Be reliably profitable, so you can make commitments and keep them. Then pursue scalability.

GET YOUR PRICING RIGHT

As I've mentioned before, many businesses fail due to under-pricing. It's not because the business owner is stupid! Rather, it's because they haven't crunched the numbers sufficiently at the beginning and haven't had systems in place to monitor profitability and know when prices needed to be tweaked.

When you start out, you need to win customers, and often the easiest-seeming strategy to do that is to price low and undercut competitors in the market. This low-price approach also overcomes another common issue that newly self-employed people wrestle with – imposter syndrome. If you have imposter syndrome, you lack confidence in the value you provide to your customers as a new business owner. As a result, you rationalise that you need to be cheaper than others in the market to deliver fair value – to not be ripping people off.

The problem with underpricing may not be immediately evident, but it manifests into a barrier to growth. The business is viable for the founder working from the kitchen table, but if they hire staff and lease some work premises, the margins vanish and they're rapidly in the red. To solve this, the business must quickly raise prices, often dislodging existing customers who were perhaps attracted to you in the first place because they were highly cost-conscious (cheapskates?).

As an illustration, let's look at the opposite of underpricing. Think about Red Bull. It's a drink that is mostly water, tastes unpleasant to most people and costs perhaps 10¢ per can to make. Yet they sell for $4 each.

Red Bull builds in a massive margin to pay for all their branding and positioning activities – from Formula One teams to crazy guys jumping out of planes looking like sugar gliders. And they built their business in a space where the ginormous marketing budgets of companies like Coke and Pepsi have crushed countless aspiring competitors in the past. Underpricing is a sure-fire way to self-employment disappointment, but Red Bull is an example of the potential when pricing is done right. (Their success also shows the power of a great marketing strategy.)

How do you ensure you avoid underpricing? There are two primary pricing strategies. You either:

1. determine your price as a function of the cost you incur to produce the product or service, or

2. determine the price with reference to the market you operate in.

The cost approach has the advantage that you can lock in an appropriate profit margin. A market approach requires less number crunching up-front, however, and can better reflect the value that you deliver. Let's explore some common methods for each approach.

Common cost pricing methods

The common cost pricing methods are as follows:

- **Cost-plus pricing**
  Here you add a fixed percentage to the cost of anything that you produce. A tradesperson installing bathroom tiles, for

instance, might simply add 50 per cent or more to the cost of the tiles.

- **Break-even pricing**
  This is typically used for physical products. You determine a minimum number of sales that you're confident you can achieve, and then set the price so that at this level of sales, all of your costs are covered – you have broken even. The goal then is to achieve sales beyond this break-even point: each subsequent sale provides your profit.

- **Target-return pricing**
  This method is often used in industries where significant investment in equipment and infrastructure is required. You determine a percentage target return that you require to make the investment in equipment worthwhile. Let's say you were a café owner, and planned on buying your own coffee roaster at a cost of $80,000, with loan repayments on the roaster charged at a 10 per cent interest rate. Given this, you might decide that it's not worth going ahead unless you'll get at least a 20 per cent return. You estimate how many packs of roasted coffee beans you will sell and the costs associated with this, then build in a 20 per cent margin per sale to ensure you hit your target return.

Common market pricing methods

Here are the common market pricing methods:

- **Going-rate pricing**
  This is an approach commonly adopted by small businesses. They simply determine their pricing with reference to what others are charging. It's easy to do and has some logic, especially for commodity-type products or services with little differentiation. Let's say you're a dishwasher installer.

If most businesses in the market charge around $150 to perform this task, then charging $500 is unlikely to see you swamped with customers – assuming there's nothing extra you offer that customers would value highly.

- **Value-added pricing**
Here, price is determined by the value you're delivering. Let's say you sell software to childcare businesses that can save their HR teams two hours per week, per staff member. Your pricing might be set based on an estimate of the dollar impact of that saving. If you calculate that your customer will save $100 per week per staff member, for instance, your price might be half of that, so that your customer is better off and you are also appropriately compensated for the value you delivered.

Making sure you make a profit

The point of getting your pricing strategy right is ensuring there is sufficient profit left for you at the end of the month. Self-employment is hard work, especially at the beginning, and it's a risk – and you lose things like paid annual leave and employer retirement benefits. To make it all worthwhile, you need to generate an appropriate profit.

Profit also provides fuel for future growth. Think back to the financial autonomy hierarchy of needs: profit gets you from the cash flow level up to building reserves. Profit is also clearly central to reliable profitability – which allows you to hire staff and make other longer-term commitments, confident in the knowledge that you'll be able to make these payments on an ongoing basis. And of course, profit is essential if you're to ever move up to the scalability phase, where you can employ others to do the work you were doing, and you're still able to draw an attractive income.

Financial autonomy in action: Blogging to gain choice

Making money from blogging is tough: many try, most fail. Sharon Gourlay, whom I spoke to in episode 41 of the podcast, has managed to crack the code.

Sharon blogged about her travels pre-kids for a long time, but no-one read her blog – except maybe her mum! In 2013, she reached a bit of a low point in her life. She and her husband were constantly working hard, yet they were only just keeping their heads above water. She decided she wanted to start an online business, using blogging as the vehicle.

Sharon described her goal as 'having choices, having freedom, living our lives how we want, where we want'. She created a new blog, *Digital Nomad Wannabe*, to record her journey, and doubled down on her travel blog to build an audience and get that commercially viable. Sharon flipped the switch in her head – it was time to become a business owner.

In 2014, after her business had been running around a year, she and her family moved to Malaysia to live the digital nomad lifestyle. The initial goal was to spend four months away, working as she went: they ended up travelling for 13 months. Sharon and her husband found that working and travelling wasn't what they wanted to do long term, though, and so after this time they moved back home. Sharon was by that time confident that she could run a successful business, however, and they had all those wonderful travel experiences under their belt.

She's since sold her original travel blog and continues to build other sites and teach others how to make money blogging. Through plenty of hard work, Sharon succeeded in her goal. She gained choice on her own terms.

SURVIVING THE STARTUP

In step 3 of your one-page business plan, you need to cover off what it will cost to deliver your product or service. Let's drill down into this now. Running your business will involve ongoing costs, of course, but the focus of this book is getting you started, so let's narrow things down for a moment to the startup phase.

I suggest breaking down your initial financial needs into two categories:

1. survival strategy
2. capital strategy.

Your survival strategy

Your survival strategy's purpose is to answer the question, 'How will I/our family survive financially while I make this transition to self-employment?' If you're undertaking this move to self-employment via a side hustle, which I encourage you to do wherever possible, then hopefully you'll continue to generate the income from your day job that you always have. So your survival strategy won't be terribly challenging. It could be you need extra childcare, or maybe you have to cut back your working hours to make time to devote to your new venture. Your survival strategy will map out your solutions to these sorts of issues.

Some moves to self-employment, however, can't be done as a side hustle. When I made the leap from employed financial planner to becoming my own boss, it wasn't possible for me to do both concurrently, given the clear conflict of interest. This is the scenario where a survival strategy becomes crucial.

In this situation, you no longer have your former income, and it will inevitably take some time before your new endeavour produces sufficient cash flow for you to draw a comparable income.

Your survival strategy might include things like reducing your mortgage repayments down to the minimum required or even switching to interest-only repayments for a while. Often couples configure things so they can live off one income, allowing the other partner to pursue self-employment in the knowledge that food will still be on the table.

For me, the solution was stretching out my final payout from my employer. When I finished up, I received a lump sum representing eight months of unused annual leave and long service leave. I worked out a plan for us to stretch this to ten months, and this provided the runway I needed to become viable. My overheads were minimal – mainly the rent on a serviced office – and I had all those covered within three months. Then, it was a case of building up the cash flow until I could get to the point of building reserves and paying myself a wage.

Your runway

I mentioned the term 'runway', and before we move onto your capital strategy, the idea deserves some fleshing out.

In my financial planning business, the normal cycle is that I have an initial meeting with a potential client, we map out the work needed and agree on a price. We get to work, present that advice and then move to implementation. Somewhere during the implementation phase, I get paid: typically I receive money in my bank account two or three months after the initial meeting.

Your self-employment plan will likely have some sort of similar cycle. Let's say you plan on baking elaborate cupcakes and, initially, selling them at local markets. Your cycle might be quite short – perhaps a week between needing to outlay money for all the ingredients and receiving the money rolling back in from sales on the weekend. At the other end of the spectrum, plenty of project work can entail an initial tendering process that can push the time between starting work and getting paid to six months or longer.

Within your plans, you need to determine what sort of runway you need in order to survive this cash-flow drought. How many months do you need to be able to support yourself before you can rely on your new business to meet your needs? From experience, I'd suggest that you take whatever your estimated time period is and produce a plan that allows it to be twice as long. Things always take longer than you hope they will when you're starting out.

What about buying a business?

I've found that people thinking about moving to self-employment as a way to gain choice often have a blind spot: the potential for buying a business. There are several key advantages to this:

- You have cash flow from day one.

- You have customers from day one.

- You acquire an asset that has proven to be commercially viable.

- You can remould the business to your vision from a position of strength.

Give some thought to whether buying a business would help you achieve your financial autonomy goal. You might want to listen to episode 4 of the Financial Autonomy podcast for more on how to analyse the financials when buying a business.

Your capital strategy

Your capital strategy answers the question, 'How will I fund this new enterprise?' Moving to self-employment typically requires some financial investment. If your self-employment pathway is in the services space (as a wedding planner, graphic designer or software engineer, for example) your capital needs will be pretty minimal – which is awesome!

Here's an example of a simple capital strategy:

- Need $15,000 to get started – to pay for a computer, software, logo design, insurance, rent, etc.

- Need $3,000 per month for the first three months to keep the doors open.

- Need $1,500 per month for the next three months (business cash flow will cover the rest).

- At six-month point, business should be generating enough income to support itself – paying for the rent, software licences, marketing, book-keeping, etc.

The checklist overleaf will help you build your capital strategy: it picks up the main expenses you're likely to face when getting your self-employment plan off the ground. I've put it in the workbook as well.

Capital strategy checklist

Expense	One-off cost	Recurring cost (monthly)
IT equipment		
Trade/profession-specific equipment		
Software		
Permits/licences		
Fit-out costs		
Business registration and set-up costs		
Logo design		
Website		
Stationery (e.g. business cards)		
Insurance		
Rent		
Employee wages (including super and tax)		
Initial stock		
Marketing		
Bank fees		
Motor vehicle expenses		
Telephone and internet		
Utilities		
Travel		
Professional development and training		
Miscellaneous expenses		
TOTAL		

ACCOUNTING BASICS

Armed with your one-page business plan and your survival and capital strategies, you're well on your way to success. However, there a few other fundamentals I want to share with you regarding bookkeeping and accounting.

Firstly, keep your business banking separate from your personal banking. I actually have my business banking with a different bank entirely, but it's not essential to go to this extreme. If your business finances are mixed in with your personal banking, you'll quickly lose track of how the business is performing, and it'll make tax and accounting extremely time-consuming and costly.

Secondly, I'd strongly advocate using some sort of accounting software package, like Xero or QuickBooks. You link your business bank account to these services and tag transactions to put them in categories, and pretty quickly the software gets to recognise the transactions and allocates them automatically for you. As well as helping with your tax obligations, these packages will give you essential insight into how your business is progressing. Here are the things that I look at every month:

- **Profit for the month**
  I generate a profit and loss report and have it show the previous three months for comparison. I look at the bottom-line number and also where the changes have been compared to previous months. If expenditure went up in a particular area, am I okay with that, or is it something I need to rein in? I break up my revenue into a few different categories, so I also look to see how these are trending.

- **Profit for the past 12 months**
  This is the same report, but instead of looking at a single month, I want to see twelve months' worth and, again, compare that to previous periods. When you get started you

won't have enough data for this, but you'll be able to look at three-month periods, for instance, after a while. This is useful, as sometimes things can be lumpy month to month, and zooming out a little provides greater perspective.

- **Debtors**

  Debtors are customers who owe you money; you've sent them an invoice and you're waiting to be paid. Disappointing though it is, many people are slow at paying, either deliberately or because they're disorganised. You are not a bank – it's not up to you to help fund your customers' cash-flow needs. Monitor your debtors closely and if people are late in paying, follow it up fast – first with a reminder invoice that payment is overdue, and then with a phone call.

- **Executive summary**

  Your software package will also likely offer some sort of executive summary, which is a report that picks up several key measurement items. This is well worth a look. Profit margin is a number I like to monitor via this report – the higher it is, the better.

Of course, I'm also always keeping an eye on our cash levels just by logging into our banking website. When running a business, the old saying 'Cash is king' holds true – think about the first stage in our hierarchy of needs, 'Cash flow'.

Financial autonomy in action: Sisters create an online empire

Sisters Jo and Tracey started their business Sistermixin (since evolved to become Additive Free Lifestyle) through a passion for healthy natural food and their concerns about the impact of additives on their family's wellbeing.

They built the business by responding to what customers were asking for and reinvesting profits. Jo had the entrepreneurial streak, while Tracey brought the implementation skills. When I spoke to them, they had progressed in just three short years from Jo posting recipes on Facebook to the business providing both of them a full-time wage. Jo's husband is now working full-time in the business as well, and it's employing three people locally and another three offshore.

They told me a key to their success was engaging a business coach. In fact, they paid for a business coach before the business was even able to generate wages for both of them. They went through several before they found the right coach, but they credit him with being a pivotal part of their success.

Check out episode 37 of the Financial Autonomy podcast to hear Jo and Tracey explain their journey.

GAINING CHOICE

Refer to your financial autonomy action plan – is self-employment a relevant pathway for the achievement of any of your goals? Self-employment can offer considerable flexibility to arrange your time to suit you. It's also the pathway that involves the greatest input and commitment from you, however – it's a lifestyle decision as much as it is a financial decision. If you haven't already, complete the third column of your action plan, 'Pathway & Strategy'.

Is self-employment your pathway to gaining choice?

Our online course 'Entrepreneur You: Transition to Self-Employment Without Going Broke' can help. Find out more at www.financialautonomy.com.au/self-employment, and use the code BOOKVIP_SELF-EMPLOYMENT to take $100 off the standard price.

WHAT ABOUT MY RETIREMENT SAVINGS?

Where do retirement savings schemes like superannuation here in Australia, 401ks in the United States and KiwiSavers in New Zealand fit into your financial autonomy plan?

Essentially, these schemes provide attractive tax incentives to encourage you to set money aside for the later years of your life. You decide how the savings are invested – whether in stocks, property, bonds and cash or some combination of these. Access to the investments is typically restricted until you are somewhere beyond age 60 and have left the workforce, which means your retirement savings won't help you gaining choice earlier in life. They are very important nonetheless for your long-term financial wellbeing.

To survive in the modern world, we need income – the days when we grew all our own food, hunted for our meat and lived a sub-sistence life are long gone. Gaining choice therefore necessitates solving the problem of how you'll generate the income you need to meet your expenses. Through this book, we've examined cash-flow strategies to optimise how your income is used, and we've explored three income-generation options – stocks, property and self-employment. Retirement savings are a tax structure through which you might choose to own stocks and property to fund your later years in a tax-friendly way. These investments generate income throughout the period of ownership, and the earnings will flow out to you once you enter retirement.

It's important to be clear in your mind what your retirement savings scheme is – it's an ownership structure. It has a specific tax treatment, with the trade-off being restricted access. It's not a substitute for stocks, property or other investment assets: it's simply a vehicle that can own these assets.

Your retirement savings' place in your plan looks like this:

Sources of income before traditional retirement age	Sources of income after traditional retirement age
Employment income	Retirement savings drawdowns
Business income	Business income
Stock dividends	Stock dividends
Property rent	Property rent

Following is a visualisation of where retirement savings fit into your plan. In the early years of adult life, all your income is derived from employment (or self-employment). You're doing something useful and being paid for it.

An example of lifetime income sources

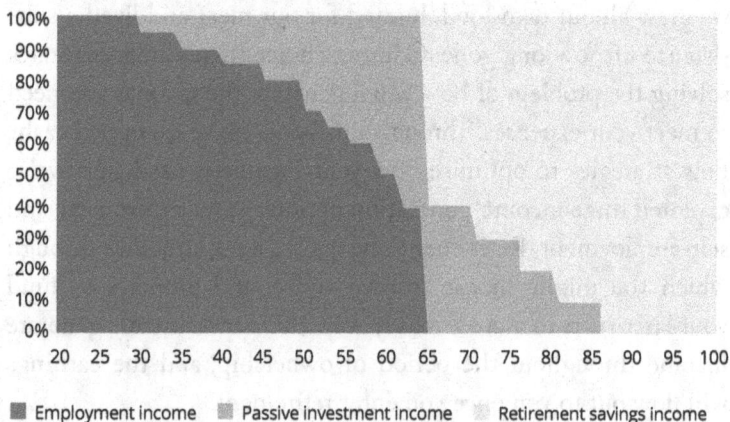

■ Employment income ■ Passive investment income ▨ Retirement savings income

Over time, you start to invest some surplus income, and your investments generate passive income in the form of dividends and/or rent. As you build on these investments, they produce increasing amounts of passive income, and this becomes an ever-larger proportion of your total income.

At some point, you give away employment or self-employment altogether. If that happens at a time when your retirement savings are accessible, as it does for most of us, you commence drawing down from your retirement savings. In the example above, I've assumed a need to draw down on the capital of your investments in retirement – that is, sell investments down. This won't be necessary for everyone.

Your financial autonomy plan is creating this passive income portion, which then creates a buffer between employment income and retirement income. It's in this area that choice is gained.

Here's how things look without financial autonomy:

Example of income sources without financial autonomy

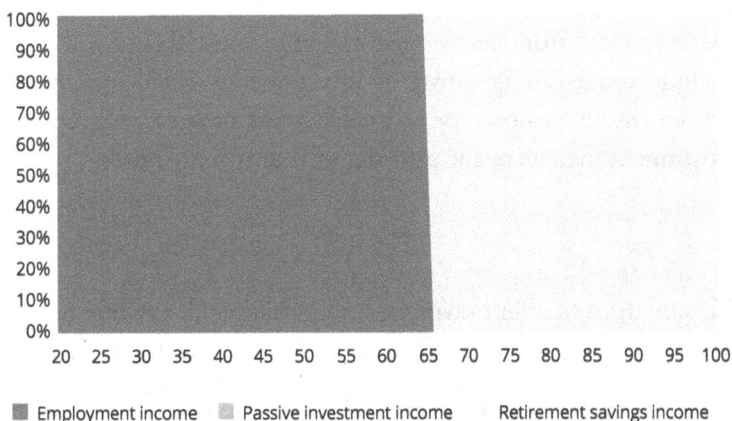

■ Employment income   ▨ Passive investment income   Retirement savings income

No passive income here – you work until you can access retirement savings. Not much choice in this life plan!

What if your goal is early retirement, perhaps retiring from the paid work force at age 50? Here's how it might look:

Early retirement income sources

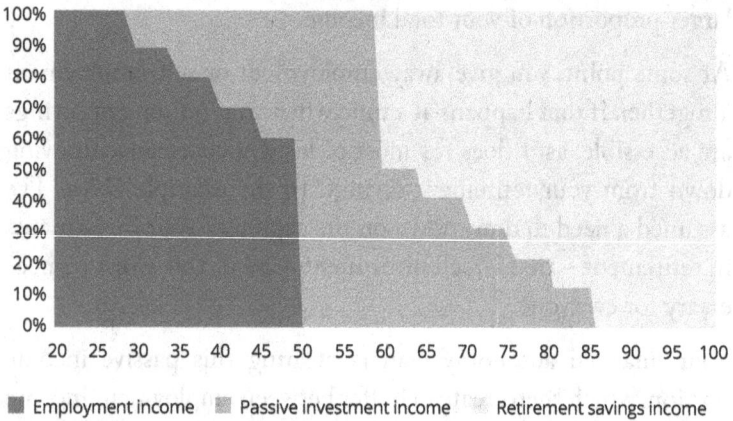

Employment income   Passive investment income   Retirement savings income

In an early retirement scenario, passive investment income provides for all your needs in between ceasing employment and gaining access to your retirement savings. (In the chart above, this occurs between ages 50 and 60, with 100 per cent of income being sourced from passive investment income. This period may include some selling down of investments.) Then, once your retirement savings become accessible, these progressively replace investment income as the provider of your income needs.

* * *

To sum up, retirement savings are important and certainly not to be neglected. They haven't been a big focus in this book, though, because when it comes to gaining choice in life, it's the passive investment income, be it from stocks, property, or a business, that provides the bulk of the choices available to you.

ACTION TIME

You've invested your valuable time in reading this book. How will you put it to use? Here's a checklist for you – what is yet to be ticked off?

☐ I determined my goals.

☐ I prioritised my goals.

☐ I put my goals into the action plan in my workbook.

☐ I defined success for me – long term and within the next three months – and added this to the action plan.

☐ I determined which pathway or pathways it makes sense to get started with.

☐ I've considered what my strategy will be within this pathway or pathways.

☐ I've chosen specific actions I will take in the next three months to make progress on my goals. (You may not do this step for every goal, but ensure you complete it for at least your number one goal.)

All these should be in your financial autonomy action plan.

Way back in chapter 1, 'Goal-setting with purpose', I talked about the value of monitoring progress when you're working on achieving important goals. If you've undertaken a weight-loss regime before, and if you've checked your weight every day, you've found that some days it goes up for no logical reason. You've been good on the food front and done your exercise, yet on some days, the results just don't tally with your efforts.

The body is a somewhat mysterious organism, and likely your bathroom scales aren't set to NASA specifications either. Who knows why it happens, but the solution is pretty simple: don't weigh yourself every day. Instead, go for once a week, or perhaps even less frequently than that.

The equivalent in the financial world is checking the value of your investments on a daily, weekly or even monthly basis. This is even more troubling than monitoring your weight, as stock markets go up and down all the time, so it is guaranteed that the value of your holdings will alter – and these fluctuations have nothing at all to do with your actions. Similarly, property valuations depend on what's been sold in the same suburb recently, and with no two properties being identical, the data is rubbery at best.

The solution, as with weight loss, is to check less often. I suggest reviewing your action plan quarterly. You could also refresh your personal balance sheet at that time if you like, though once or twice a year for this is enough.

FINANCIAL AUTONOMY JOURNEY EXAMPLES

If you still need a bit of encouragement to burst out of the blocks into your financial autonomy journey, here are some examples of how things can unfold, starting with my own.

My journey to financial autonomy

Stocks	Property	Self-employment	Comments
Accumulated stocks in my teens and early twenties.			
	1996: 1st property (small and ugly apartment)		Sold my stocks to provide the deposit.
Acquired stocks as cash flow permitted – ongoing.	**1999:** 2nd property (family home)		Sold 1st property, joined forces with partner (now wife).
		2005: resigned from my job, became self-employed as a financial planner.	Cash-flow management extremely important in early years.
		2008: acquired a financial-planning business from a retiring planner.	Equity built up in home essential for obtaining the loan to make this acquisition possible.
	2010: purchased office premises.		Purchased via retirement savings. Lease these premises to my financial-planning business.
	2020: purchased small apartment – pure investment.		Equity in home helped maximise this opportunity.

I've used all three pathways at various times in life, and right now I have all three in play.

Kate's journey to financial autonomy

Stocks	Property	Self-employment	Comments
Started investing in ETFs in twenties.			Still packed in plenty of travel.
		Job got cut back to 2 days per week, so started freelancing and picking up contract work as a graphic designer.	Sold some stocks when cash got tight in the early days.
		Employed position wound down but continued to engage her on a contract basis as needed.	
Buying ETFs again – sustainability-themed usually – when surplus cash flow allows.			Now full-time contractor. Happy renting for time being – likes the flexibility.

Kate has successfully gained choice via the stocks and self-employment pathways, at a relatively young age.

John and Lesley's journey to financial autonomy

Stocks	Property	Self-employment	Comments
	Bought first home together.		Accumulated deposit via bank savings.
	Home became a rental property.		John got an overseas posting. Spent the next 12 years away.
Bought stocks intermittently.			Used savings capacity to pay off home loan and build some investments.
	Bought new home.		Returned to Australia. Kept original home as a rental and bought a new home for themselves.
Continued buying stocks here and there.	Bought a small apartment for investment purposes.		Career going well and income significant.
Added to retirement savings and bought predominantly stocks.			Received an inheritance.
	Bought another investment property.		The 2 investment properties were providing positive cash flow, so bought another.

John is about five years out from his preferred retirement date, though financially he could retire tomorrow if he wished.

Thanks for working your way through my book. It reflects 30 years of experience and learning, both directly and through the many wonderful clients I've had the privilege of working with.

The COVID-19 pandemic has highlighted how quickly our world can change, and gaining choice has never been more important – it could be thought of as resiliency. I hope the ideas you've learned from these pages help you live a happy and fulfilling life, and insulate you financially from the turmoil the world can sometimes throw at us.

WANT MORE?

Here are some other ways I can help you and which are important to you gaining choice in life:

- **The podcast** – the Financial Autonomy podcast is available on all of the usual platforms, with a catalogue of over 150 episodes.

- **Our weekly newsletter** – *Gaining CHOICE* has need-to-knows, plus some brain food for the curious. Subscribe at www.financialautonomy.com.au/gainingchoice.

- **Online courses** – Financial Autonomy Academy provides a deeper dive into specific strategies to enable you to gain choice in your life. Take a look at financial-autonomy.teachable.com.

- **Workshops and presentations** – I regularly deliver corporate workshops for teams and professional associations throughout Australia. Current workshop topics include:
  - *Money Mastery: De-Stress Your Finances and Gain Choice in Life* (two versions – 2 hours or 45 minutes)
  - *Financial Autonomy – converting your hard work into life choices* (two versions – 2 hours or 45 minutes)
  - *Money and Happiness* (45 minutes).

To discuss your needs, email **contact@guidancefs.com.au** or ask your personnel department to contact me.

Public workshop dates are promoted through the *Gaining CHOICE* weekly email newsletter.

ABOUT THE AUTHOR

Paul Benson has been providing financial planning advice for more than 20 years, initially as an employee of one of Australia's major banks, and since 2005 as the principal of his own firm.

Paul's passion for financial independence comes from working with clients over so many years: seeing the different journeys of people's lives, what brings them happiness, and what causes stress and worry.

Paul launched his Financial Autonomy podcast in 2017. Initially it was produced entirely as a family affair – Paul recorded the audio, his son created the theme music and did the editing, and his wife provided the outro. Today Financial Autonomy is one of the most popular personal finance podcasts in Australia.

Paul holds a Bachelor of Business in Economics and Finance, and is a Certified Financial Planner.

When not thinking about finances, Paul enjoys family time with his wife and two teenage sons. He loves playing board games – Settlers of Catan being a particular favourite – running, orienteering, and getting down to Williamstown beach during the warmer months for an ocean swim.

SOURCES

Delmendo, L.C., 'Japan's Shrinking Population is Producing a Surplus of Housing', *Global Property Guide*, 25 March 2020, www.globalpropertyguide.com/Asia/Japan/Price-History.

Goldsmith, B., 'Goals are a Relationship Necessity. Here are 10 Tools to Help', *Psychology Today*, 6 October 2010.

Guillebeau, C., *Side Hustle*, Currency, New York, 2017.

Kobayashi, M., 'The Housing Market and Housing Policies in Japan', Asian Development Bank Institute working paper no. 558, March 2016, www.adb.org/sites/default/files/publication/181404/adbi-wp558.pdf.

Lin, Y., Ma, Z., Zhao, K., Hu, W. & J. Wei, 'The Impact of Population Migration on Urban Housing Prices: Evidence from China's Major Cities', *Sustainability*, no. 10, 2018, p. 3169.

Portnoy, B., *The Geometry of Wealth*, Harriman House Ltd, Petersfield, UK, 2018.

Raser-Rowland, A. & A. Grubb, *The Art of Frugal Hedonism*, Melliodora Publishing, Hepburn, Australia, 2016.

Ries, E., *The Lean Startup*, Penguin UK, London, 2011.

Sethi, R., *I Will Teach You to Be Rich*, Workman Publishing, New York, 2009.

Stanley, S. & W. Danko, *The Millionaire Next Door*, Taylor Trade Publishing, Lanham, Maryland, USA, 2010.

The Investment Funds Institute of Canada, 'The History of Mutual Funds', www.ific.ca/en/articles/who-we-are-history-of-mutual-funds.

Urban, T., 'The AI Revolution: the Road to Superintelligence', *Wait But Why*, 22 January 2015, waitbutwhy.com/2015/01/artificial-intelligence-revolution-1.html

INDEX

401k 187
50/20/30 method 51-52

accountancy fees 122
accounting 183
Acorns 65
Additive Free Lifestyle 184
affordability 131
agents' fees 142
aggressive investment 95,
 137
Airbnb 153
altruistic goals 19
annual fees 44
apartments 127, 133
apps 59, 64
Art of Frugal Hedonism,
 The 34
artificial intelligence (AI)
 21-22
asset allocation 86-87
Attenborough, David 35
Australian Bureau of
 Statistics 57
automated bank transfers 29,
 53, 56, 142

balanced investor 94
bank accounts 51-52, 53,
 54, 56
bear market 77
behavioural finance 75-77, 97
big cut strategy 57
bills 53, 54, 55, 62
blogs 1, 177
body corporate costs 120, 127
Bogle, Jack 82
bonds 86, 87, 190
books 1, 7
borrowing 111-116, 135
borrowing to buy stocks
 97-99
brokerage accounts 81
brokers 81-82
bucket strategy 53-55
budgeting 33
 – rethinking 36
 – strategy 45
 – the right strategy for you
  50
budgets, why most fail 62-64
Buffett, Warren 69, 95, 148
building defects 133

bull market 77
business plan 158-162
buying a business 180

capital strategy 181-182
career change 19, 36-37
Career Emporium 156
cash 86, 87, 184
cash flow 4, 33-45, 110, 122,
   131, 137, 170, 180
   – management self-
     assessment 49 -50
   – plan 36
   – strategy 38, 42
   – surplus 60, 110
Cavendish, John 164-165
change 19, 20
Chime 65
choice 4, 5, 19, 101, 102, 144,
   147, 185
city properties 128
Coke 174
commercial property 128-129
commodities 87
Commonwealth Bank 65, 73
competition 96
confirmation bias 76
conflict 8
conscious spending 37
conservative investing 94
core-satellite investing 92-93
corporate bonds 87
council rates 119

COVID-19 74, 97, 147, 196
credit cards 43-45
CSR 72
cutting expenses 42

Danko, William 43
debt 44, 45, 106, 126
debtors 184
debt repayment 51, 52
defensive assets 87
demand 127
developers 127
Digital Nomad Wannabe 177
discipline 56, 63
Disneyland 22, 24
diversification 74, 77, 78-80
dividends 70, 71, 74, 188, 189
dividend yield 88, 91, 92
doubling investment returns
   94-95
Dyson, James 149
Dyson vacuum cleaners 153

early retirement 42
earnings per share (EPS) 89
employment income 188
entrepreneurship 7
equity 126
exchange traded funds
   (ETFs) 69, 79, 80, 81,
   82-84, 87, 93
executing a plan 15
executive summary 184

expenses 34-35, 41, 57
experience goals 18

Facebook 185
family holidays 22, 24
Ferrari, Enzo 155
financial autonomy action
    plan 27, 28-29, 125
financial autonomy
    framework 3
financial autonomy goals
    28-29, 129
financial autonomy journey
    examples 192-196
financial autonomy pathways
    9-10
Financial Autonomy podcast
    34, 73, 163, 197
Financial Autonomy
    workbook 6
financial independence 5
financial security 5, 33
fixed interest rate loans 117
flexibility 15
food 57
Fulfillment By Amazon
    (FBA) 164-165
fund managers 82

Gates, Bill 5
gearing 73, 98, 112, 114-115
Geometry of Wealth, The 75, 85
global financial crisis 74, 147

global stocks 87
goals 2, 4, 16-17, 22-23, 27,
    63, 191
    – categories of 18-19
goal-setting 13-15
Goldsmith, Dr Barton 19
Google 155
Gourlay, Sharon 177
growth 91
    – assets 87
    – rates 132
    – stocks 93
Guillebeau, Chris 160

happiness 4, 13-14
herding bias 76
hierarchy of needs 168-169
high-income-earners 43, 52
household budgets 57
houses 127
housing 58
how much money do you
    need to live? 42-43
hybrids 87

idea validation 152-155
IKEA furniture 155
imitation 155
income 8, 9, 34, 40, 41, 88,
    126, 132, 188, 190
    – maximising 4, 41
income-earning capacity 43
index funds 82, 83

industry sectors 79
inflation 108
infrastructure 87, 134
ING 65
insurance 120
interest-free period 44
interest-only loans 116, 126
interest rates 109, 113, 117,
    118, 140
investing vs trading 95-96
investment property 8
investment strategy 4, 70
investment time frame 86
I Will Teach You to Be Rich 37

jobs 141
jobs and industry 134

Kickstarter campaigns 155
KiwiSavers 187

laddering approach 108
land tax 119-120
Lean Startup, The 154
Lee, Ruby 156-157
leverage 98, 112
liquidity 74, 98
loan repayments 110, 115,
    118, 135
loans 115-117
long-term investor 96
long-term strategy 106
Lorne Pier to Pub race 14

maintenance costs 120,
    121, 127
managed funds 82, 83
marketing commissions 132
marketing plan 158
Maslow's hierarchy of needs
    168-169
Massachusetts Investors Trust
    82
Microsoft 155
millionaire households 43
Millionaire Next Door,
    The 43
minimalist movement 2
minimum viable product 154
Mint app 64
money habits 59, 60
money management 48
MoneySmart website 54
Moore's law 21
multi-property investment
    strategy 125-126
multi-property investor
    143-144
musicians 6
must-haves 51, 52
mutual funds 82

negative gearing 136-138
negotiating a raise 41
net asset position 25, 26
new estate property 132

New York Stock Exchange (NYSE) 80
no-budget strategy 59

offset accounts 57, 138-139
offset account vs extra repayments 138
off-the-plan property 132
online broking 82
origin stories 160-161
overspending 44, 45
owner-occupier property 127
owners corporation fees 127

passive income 5, 41, 105, 116-117, 137, 188, 189
pay yourself first 55
Penn, Joanna 163-164
Pepsi 174
PE ratio 88, 89, 90-91, 92
personal balance sheet 25
Pocketbook 64
PocketSmith 64
podcasts 7
population growth 143
portfolio constructions 79
Portnoy, Brian 75, 85
positive cash flow 110
prerequisites, for goals 26
price growth 132-133
pricing 158, 161, 173-174
  – break-even 175
  – cost-plus pricing 174
  – going-rate 175-176
  – target-return 175
  – value-added 176
principal and interest loan 115-117, 126
prioritising goals 22-24
private equity 87
procrastination 162
product offering 159
profit 70, 176, 183-184
profitability 171
promotion at work 41
property 5, 34, 87, 98, 190
  – cash flow 105
  – growth 106-107
  – location 134
  – maintenance 142
  – manager fees 121
  – managers 139
  – selection 125-131
  – types 126
property investing
  – costs of 119-121
  – managing the risk 140
property-investment cash-flow plan 122-123
property-investment self-assessment 129-131
property investment strategy 106-107, 125
Psychology Today 19

Qapital 65
QuickBooks 183

Raiz 65
Ramsey, David 60
Raser-Roland, Annie 34-35
recency bias 76
recreation 58
Red Bull 174
redundancy package 36
regional properties
reinvestment 71
relationship goals 19-20
renovating 22, 24, 129
rental income 106, 109, 110,
   123, 126, 135, 188
rental-income strategy
   108-109
reserves 170
residential property 128
resilience 21, 170
retirement 2, 22, 24, 35
retirement savings 187-190
retraining 21, 41
reverse budget strategy 55-57
Ries, Eric 149, 154
risk 15, 97, 98, 113
risk tolerance 87
rounding apps 65
runway 179

S&P 500 75, 82
S&P/ASX 200 77

savings 45, 47, 138, 190
   – account 54
   – capacity 7
   – plan 72
   – rate 38-40, 63, 64
savings vs debt 119
scalability 172-173
second job 58
self-assessment 7, 49, 130
self-employment 5-6, 15, 34,
   41, 147, 148, 149, 169, 178,
   189
self-employment strategy 157
self-employment, transition
   to 149, 152
selling your business 101
setbacks 15
Sethi, Ramit 37
short-term speculator 96
Side Hustle 160
side hustles 148-149, 150-
   151, 152, 178
Sinek, Simon 14
single-property investing
   strategy 126-127
Sistermixin 184-185
SMART goals 17-18
speculative companies 77
speculative investing 97, 99
spending 37, 56
   – calculating 53, 54
   – more than you earn 33
   – plans 60

stamp duty 142
Stanley, Thomas 43
startup, surviving the 178-180
Start With Why 14
statistics 111
stockbrokers 81-82, 83
stock market facts 77
stock markets 80
stocks 4-5, 7, 8, 34, 69-83,
   190
   – are they risky? 73-74
   – domestic 87
   – global 87
   – historical performance
     of 74
   – how they make money
     71-72
   – income 72
   – price growth of 71
   – price movements 75
   – price volatility 75
   – selection 93
strata fees 120
success 2, 27, 34, 161-162
support network 170-171
surplus cash 7
SurveyMonkey 159

tax 96, 119, 137
TED Talks 14
tenants 133, 140-141
'things' goals 19
tracking your spending 59-61
   – apps 59
transport 58

unexpected expenses 63
Up 65
utilities 121

vacancy periods 121-122, 128
valuation-growth strategy
   107-108
Vanguard 83
variable-rate loans 117

wants 51, 52
why, finding your 14-15, 16

Xero 183

yield 135-136

zero-based budgeting 45,
   60-62

NOTES

NOTES

NOTES

NOTES

NOTES

NOTES

NOTES

NOTES